IMAGES OF WAR

Schnellbootwaffe

Adolf Hitler's Guerrilla War at Sea

S-Boote 1939–45

*To all sailors in history who sailed
and fought for their homeland*

IMAGES OF WAR

Schnellbootwaffe

Adolf Hitler's Guerrilla War at Sea

S-Boote 1939–45

RARE PHOTOGRAPHS FROM WARTIME ARCHIVES

HRVOJE SPAJIĆ

Pen & Sword

MILITARY

AN IMPRINT OF PEN & SWORD BOOKS LTD.
YORKSHIRE – PHILADELPHIA

First published in Great Britain in 2021 by
PEN & SWORD MILITARY
An imprint of
Pen & Sword Books Ltd
Yorkshire - Philadelphia

ISBN 978 1 39909 175 6

Typeset in 12/14.5 Gill Sans by SJmagic DESIGN SERVICES, India.

Printed and bound in England by CPI Group (UK) Ltd., Croydon

Pen & Sword Books Ltd. incorporates the Imprints of Pen & Sword Archaeology, Atlas, Aviation, Battleground, Discovery, Family History, History, Maritime, Military, Naval, Politics, Railways, Select, Transport, True Crime, Fiction, Frontline Books, Leo Cooper, Praetorian Press, Seaforth Publishing, Wharncliffe and White Owl.

For a complete list of Pen & Sword titles please contact

PEN & SWORD BOOKS LIMITED
47 Church Street, Barnsley, South Yorkshire, S70 2AS, England
E-mail: enquiries@pen-and-sword.co.uk
Website: www.pen-and-sword.co.uk

Or

PEN AND SWORD BOOKS
1950 Lawrence Rd, Havertown, PA 19083, USA
E-mail: uspen-and-sword@casematepublishers.com
Website: www.penandswordbooks.com

Contents

Tables

1. Rank equivalents

KzS Kapitän zur See	Commander
FK Fregattenkapitän	Frigate Captain
KK Korvettenkapitän	Corvette Captain
KL Kapitänleutnant	Lieutenant Commander
OL Oberleutnant	First Lieutenant
Lt Leutnant	Second Lieutenant
LI Leitender Ingenieur	Chief Engineer
Fähnrich	Ensign
Diesel Obermaschimist	Chief Machinist
Dieselgast	Diesel Machinist
Funkmaat	Radio Officer
Bootmaat	Warrant Officer
Torpedomaat	Torpedo Officer
Matrosengefreiter	Seaman First Class

2. Composition of the flotillas (1941)

1st "S-Boote" flotilla		
Fleet leader:	Kptlt.	Heinz Birnbacher
"S-26"	Oblt. z. S.	Kurt Fimmen
"S-27"	Oblt. z. S.	Hermann Büchting
"S-28"	Oblt. z. S.	Bernd Klug
"S-29"	Oblt. z. S.	Götz Friedrich Götz von Mirbach
"S-101"	Oblt. z. S.	Georg-Stuhr Christiansen
"S-102"	Oblt. z. S.	Werner Toniges

2nd "S-Boote" flotilla		
Fleet leader:	Korv. kpt.	Rudolph Petersen
"S-30"	Oblt. z. S.	Klaus Feldt
"S-33"	Lt. z. S.	Paul Popp
"S-34"	Oblt. z. S.	Albrecht Obermaier
"S-36"	Oblt. z. S.	Wolf-Dietrich Babbel
"S-55"	Oblt. z. S.	Hermann Opdenhoff
"S-56"	Oblt. z. S.	Wilhelm Meentzen
"S-201"	Oblt. z. S.	Ullrich Roeder

3rd "S-Boote" flotilla		
Fleet leader:	Kptlt.	Friedrich Kemnade
"S-54"	Lt. z. S.	Herbert Wagner
"S-57"	Lt. z. S.	Güntger Erdmann
"S-58"	Lt. z. S.	Eberhard Geiger
"S-59"	Lt. z. S.	Heinz Haag
"S-60"	Oblt. z. S.	Siegfried Wuppermann

4th "S-Boote" flotilla (still training in Germany)		
Fleet leader:	Kptlt.	Niels Bätge
"S-11"	Lt. z. S.	Erwin Lüders
"S-22"	Oblt. z. S.	Bogislav Priebe
"S-24"	Lt. z. S.	Hans Joachim Stöve
"S-25"	Oblt. z. S.	Karl Schneider

3. German battle order on the Western Front (1942)

2nd "S-Boote" Flotilla		
Fleet leader:	Kptlt. Feldt.	Rudolph Petersen
"S-29"	Kptlt.	Manfred Schmidt
"S-39"	Kptlt.	Felix Zymalkowski
"S-53" ·	Oblt. z. S.	Peter Block
"S-62"	Oblt. z. S.	Hermann Opdenhoff
"S-70"	Oblt. z. S.	Hans Helmut Klose
"S-103"	No named commander	

"S-104"	Oblt. z. S.	Ulrich Roeder
"S-105"	Lt. z. S.	Künzel (later Hans-Joachim Wrampe)
"S-111"	Oblt. z. S.	Paul Popp

4th "S-Boote" Flotilla		
Fleet leader:	Kptlt.	Niels Bätge
"S-48"	Oblt. z. S.	Götz Friedrich von Mirbach
"S-49"	Oblt. z. S.	Max Günther
"S-50"	Oblt. z. S.	Karl-Eberhard Karcher
"S-51"	Oblt. z. S.	Hans Jürgen Meyer
"S-52"	Oblt. z. S.	Karl Müller
"S-64"	Oblt. z. S.	Friedrich Wihem Wilcke
"S-109"	Oblt. z. S.	Helmut Dross
"S-110"	Oblt. z. S.	Albert Causemann
"S-107"	(not yet in service)	

6th "S-Boote" Flotilla		
Fleet leader:	Kptlt.	Albrecht Obermaier
"S-18"	Oblt. z. S.	Heinz-Friedrich Nitsche
"S-19"	Lt. z. S.	Wolfgang Höming
"S-20"	Oblt. z. S.	Gerhard Meyering
"S-22"	Oblt. z. S.	Herbert Witt
"S-24"	Oblt. z. S.	Heinz Nolte
"S-69"	Oblt. z. S.	August Licht
"S-71"	Oblt. z. S.	Friedrich Wihelm Jopping
"S-101"	Lt. z. S.	Jürgen Goetschke

4. Organization of the Schnellbootwaffe in February 1945

Leader of the S-Bootwaffe: Kommodore Rudolf Petersen
Chief of Staff: Korvettenkapitän Heinrich Erdmann

1st flotilla
Leader: Korvettenkapitän Hermann Büchtig
"S-216": Kapitänleutnant Ernst-August Seevers
"S-225": Oberleutnant zur See Gërhard Behrens
"S-707": Oberleutnant zur See Peter Neumeier

2nd flotilla
Leader: Korvettenkapitän Hermann Opdenhoff
"S-174": Oberleutnant zur See Hugo Wendler
"S-176": Oberleutnant zur See Friedrich Stockfleth
"S-177": Oberleutnant zur See Karl Boseniuk
"S-181": Oberleutnant zur See Martin Schlenk
"S-209": Oberleutnant zur See Kurt Neugebauer
"S-210": Oberleutnant zur See Günter Weisheit
"S-221": Oberleutnant zur See Schneider

4th flotilla
Leader: Korvettenkapitän Kurt Fimmen
"S-201": Obstrm. Wilhem Kohrt
"S-202": Kapitänleutnant Joachim Wiencke
"S-204": Reserve Leutnant zur See Claus Hinrichs
"S-205": Oberleutnant zur See Hans Neuburger
"S-219": Oberleutnant zur See Dietrich Howaldt
"S-220": Kapitänleutnant Helmut Dross
"S-703": Reserve Oberleutnant zur See Dieter Steinhauer

5th flotilla
Leader: Kapitänleutnant Hermann Holzapfel
"S-67": Leutnant zur See Heiko Buddecke
"S-85": Leutnant zur See Hans-L. Reimers
"S-92": Oberleutnant zur See Fritz Schay
"S-98": Leutnant zur See Heinrich Horkisch
"S-110": Oberleutnant zur See Johann Schmölzer
"S-127": Oberleutnant zur See Hinrich Ahrens
"S-132": Obstrm. Heinz Deppe

6th flotilla
Leader: Kapitänleutnant Hens Matzen
"S-211": Oberleutnant zur See August Licht
"S-212": Obstrm. Alfred Schannow
"S-213": Leutnant zur See Reinhard Bucher

"S-222": Leutnant zur See Breithaupt
"S-223": Oberleutnant zur See Enno Brandi
"S-704": Oberleutnant zur See Georg Korn
"S-705": Kapitänleutnant Hans Karl Hemmer
"S-706": Oberleutnant zur See Wilhelm Waldhausen

8th flotilla

Leader: Korvettenkapitän Felix Zymalkowski

"S-193": Under repair
"S-194": Kapitänleutnant Siegrfried Wörmcke
"S-195": Kapitänleutnant Walter Knapp
"S-196": Oberleutnant zur See Günter Rathenow
"S-197": Oberleutnant zur See Wulff Fanger
"S-199": Oberleutnant zur See Horst Schuur
"S-701": Oberleutnant zur See Ulrich Toermer

9th flotilla

Leader: Korvettenkapitän Götz Friedrich von Mirbach

"S-130": Kapitänleutnant Günter Rabe
"S-167": Leutnant zur See Seifert
"S-168": Oberleutnant zur See Dau
"S-175": Oberleutnant zur See Franz Behr
"S-206": Kapitänleutnant Ulrich Roeder
"S-207": Oberleutnant zur See Hans Schirren
"S-214": Oberleutnant zur See Rudolph Beck
"S-112": Leutnant zur See Nikelowski

10th flotilla

Leader: Kapitänleutnant Dietrich Bludau

"S-186": Oberleutnant zur See Ludwig Ritter
"S-191": Leutnant zur See Günther Benja
"S-215": Oberleutnant zur See Heinz-Dieter Mohs
"S-224": Leutnant zur See Bruno Klockow

11th flotilla
Leader: Kapitänleutnant Nikolai Baron von Stempel
"S-170": Obstrm. Odermann
"S-208": Obstrm. Mauroschat
Support ship: *Tanga*
Commander: Oberleutnant zur See Johann Wortmann

1st S-Boote division
Division leader: Fregattenkapitän Herbert Schultz
3rd S-Boote flotilla
Leader: Kapitänleutnant Günther Schultz

Group 1
Group leader: Oberleutnant zur See Günther Milbradt
"S-30": Oberleutnant zur See Gunnar Kelm
"S-36": Leutnant zur See Rudolf Svoboda
"S-61": Oberleutnant zur See Jürgen Hardtke

Group 2 (former 7th flotilla)
Group leader: Oberleutnant zur See Hans-Georg Buschmann
"S-151": Leutnant zur See Helmuth Greiner
"S-152": Obstrm. Erich Mensch
"S-153": Oberleutnant zur See Hans Wulf Heckel
"S-154": Obstrm. Erwin Schipke
"S-156": Reserve Oberleutnant zur See Marxen
"S-157": Oberleutnant zur See Hans-Ulrich Liebhold

Group 3 (former 24th flotilla)
Group leader: Oberleutnant zur See Hermann Bollenhagen
"S-621": Oberleutnant zur See Wernicke
"S-623": Oberleutnant zur See Elksneit
"S-626": Leutnant zur See Klaus Burba
"S-627": Leutnant zur See Paul Overwaul
"S-628": Under repair

"S-629": Leutnant zur See Ernst-Günter Müller	
"S-630": Oberleutnant zur See Cartagna (Italian crew)	

S-Boote Training Division
Division leader: Korvettankapitän Klaus Feldt
Support ship: *Buea*
Commander: Oberleutnant zur See Ludwig Stölzer
Support ship: *Hermann-von-Wissmann*
Commander: Oberleutnant zur See Gert Vassel

1st training flotilla
Leader: Kapitänleutnant Friedrich-Wilhelm Wilcke
"S-62": Oberleutnant zur See Hermann Rost
"S-79": Oberleutnant zur See Hermann Zeiler
"S-89": Oberleutnant zur See Jasper Osterloh
"S-90": Reserve Leutnant zur See Gärbers
"S-109": Reserve Leutnant zur See Koppermeck
"S-133": Leutnant zur See Günter Schiersmann
Support ship: *Adolf-Lüderitz*
Commander: Oberleutnant zur See August Gauland

2nd training flotilla
Leader: Kapitänleutnant Hans-Helmut Klose
"S-64": Oberleutnant zur See Karl Deckert
"S-69": Leutnant zur See Eberhard Runge
"S-76": Oberleutnant zur See Wildner
"S-81": Oberleutnant zur See Bernhard Wülfing
"S-83": Oberleutnant zur See Carl Hoffman
"S-99": Leutnant zur See Nienstedt
"S-117": Oberleutnant zur See Hans-Viltor Howaldt
"S-135": Oberleutnant zur See Hans-Jürgen Schwepcke
Support ship: *Tsingtau*
Commander: Oberleutnant zur See Kurt Kmetsch

3rd training flotilla
Leader: Kapitänleutnant Hans Detlefsen
"S-21", "S-22", "S-24", "S-25", "S-65", "S-68", "S-82", "S-95", "S-97", "S-101", "S-103", "S-105", "S-107", "S-108", "S-113", "S-116", "S-118", "S-120", "S-122", "S-123"
Support ship: *Carl-Peters*
Commander: Oberleutnant zur See Walter Reuthal
The three training flotillas were stationed in the Baltic Sea.

Maps

Operations in the English Channel (1941–44)

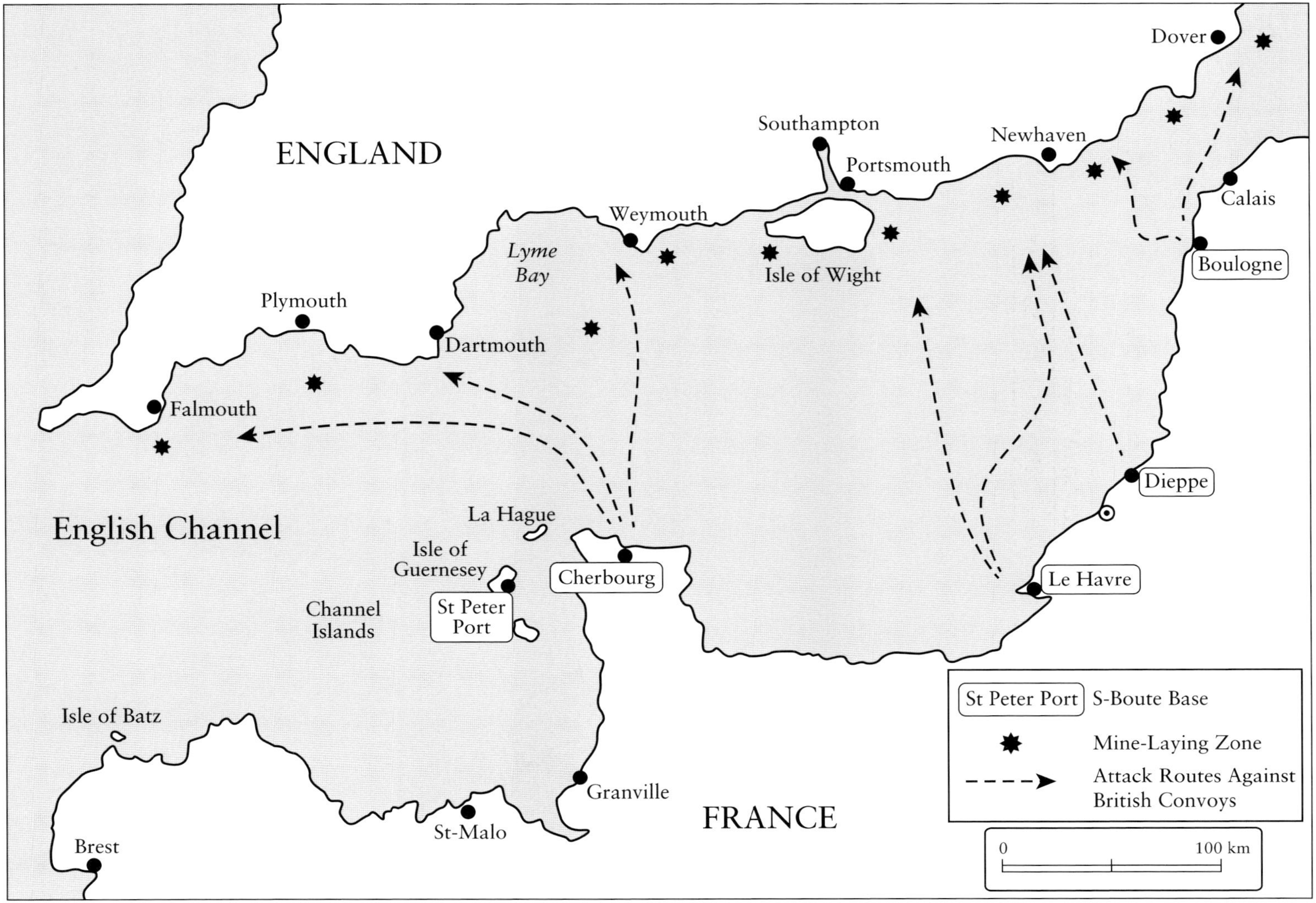

ENGLAND

FRANCE

English Channel

Dover
Calais
Boulogne
Dieppe
Le Havre
Newhaven
Portsmouth
Southampton
Isle of Wight
Weymouth
Lyme Bay
Dartmouth
Plymouth
Falmouth
Cherbourg
La Hague
Isle of Guernesey
St Peter Port
Channel Islands
Granville
St-Malo
Isle of Batz
Brest

Legend:

St Peter Port | S-Boute Base

Mine-Laying Zone

Attack Routes Against British Convoys

0 — 100 km

Operations in the North Sea (1941–44)

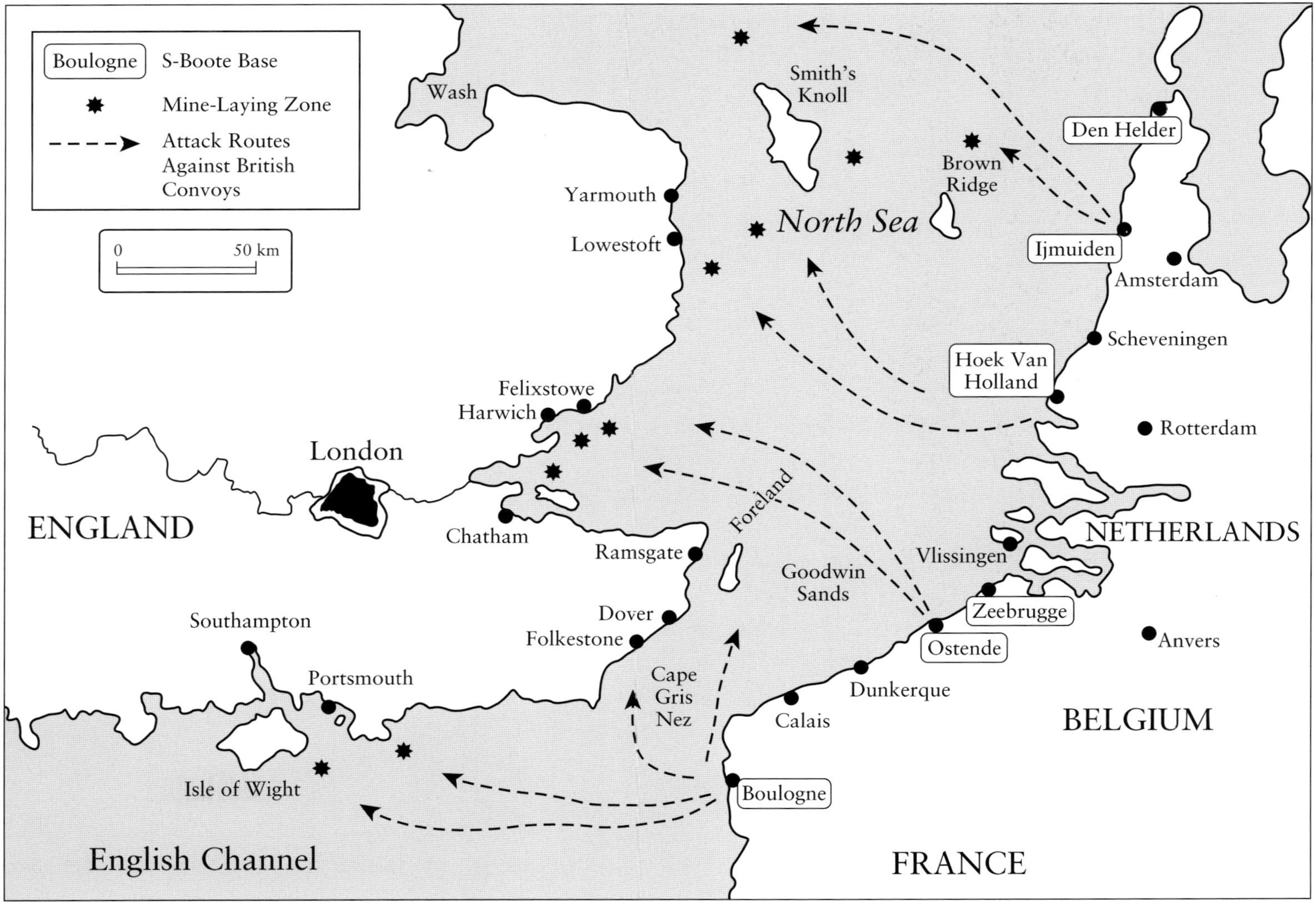

Legend:

Boulogne	S-Boote Base
✴	Mine-Laying Zone
– – –▶	Attack Routes Against British Convoys

0 ——— 50 km

Labels on map:

NETHERLANDS

BELGIUM

FRANCE

ENGLAND

North Sea

English Channel

Den Helder

Ijmuiden

Amsterdam

Scheveningen

Rotterdam

Hoek Van Holland

Anvers

Zeebrugge

Vlissingen

Ostende

Dunkerque

Calais

Boulogne

Brown Ridge

Smith's Knoll

Goodwin Sands

Foreland

Yarmouth

Lowestoft

Felixstowe

Harwich

Chatham

Ramsgate

Dover

Folkestone

Cape Gris Nez

London

Wash

Southampton

Portsmouth

Isle of Wight

16

Final operations in the North Sea (1945)

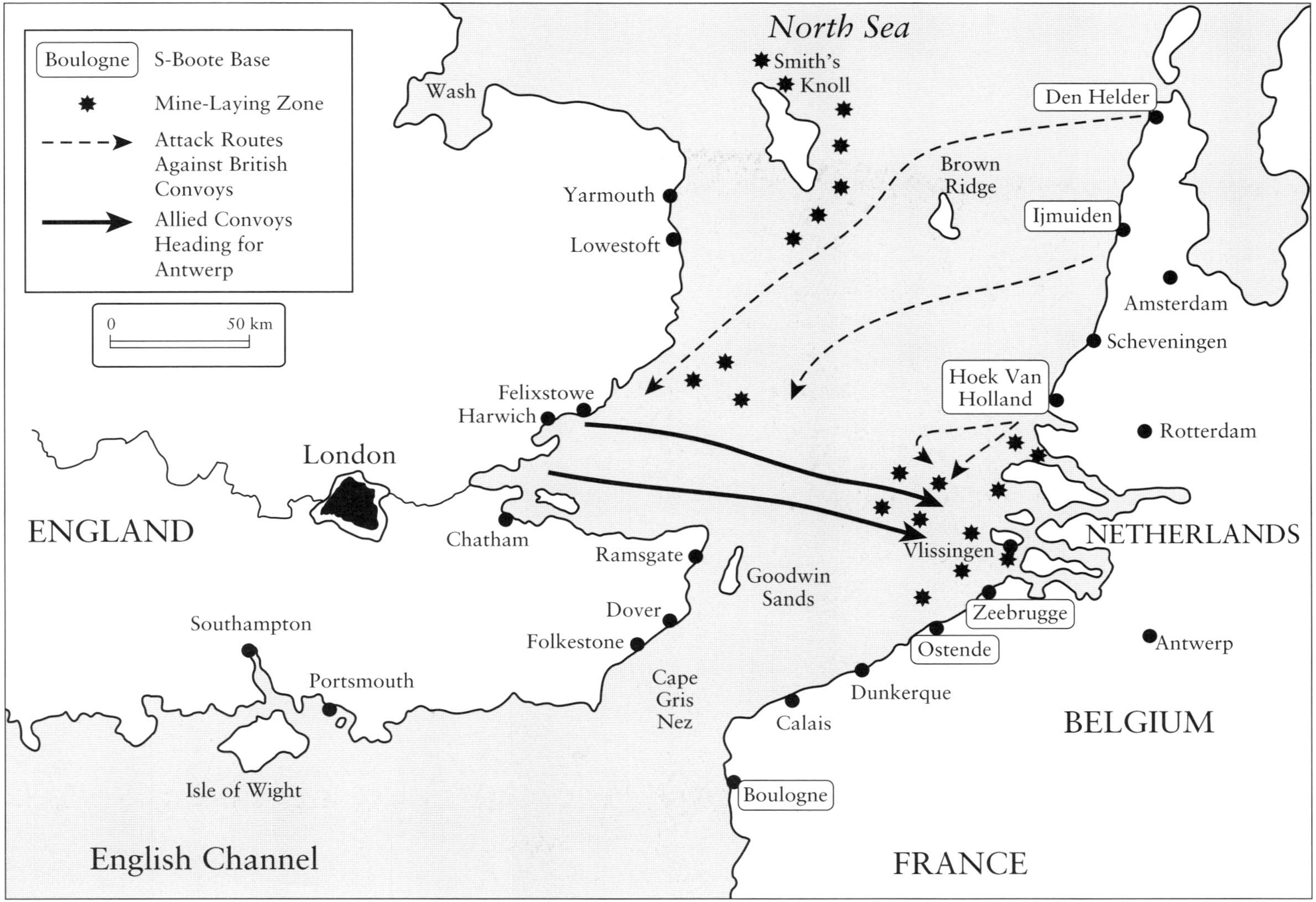

North Sea

NETHERLANDS

BELGIUM

FRANCE

ENGLAND

English Channel

Amsterdam

Scheveningen

Rotterdam

Antwerp

Den Helder

Ijmuiden

Hoek Van Holland

Zeebrugge

Vlissingen

Ostende

Dunkerque

Calais

Boulogne

Brown Ridge

Smith's Knoll

Yarmouth

Lowestoft

Felixstowe

Harwich

Chatham

Ramsgate

Dover

Folkestone

Cape Gris Nez

Goodwin Sands

London

Wash

Southampton

Portsmouth

Isle of Wight

Legend:

Boulogne — S-Boote Base

✳ — Mine-Laying Zone

⇠ (dashed arrow) — Attack Routes Against British Convoys

⬆ (solid arrow) — Allied Convoys Heading for Antwerp

0 — 50 km

17

Illustrations

Schnellboote "S-1"

The "S-1" in 1932. Two years earlier this torpedo boat was completed and named "UZ-16", before being renamed "W-1" on 31 March 1931. The "S-1" was 27 metres long, with a displacement of 40.4 tons when fully loaded, and was driven by three 12-cylinder 900-hp Daimler Benz BFz gasoline engines, along with an additional 100-hp Maybach "cruise" engine. This torpedo boat could reach 34 knots at full speed, and its armament was made up of two 533-mm torpedo launching tubes, with four torpedoes, and a 7.92mm-calibre machine gun. The crew was composed of an officer and thirteen seamen. On 16 March 1932, the gun boat joined the 1st *S-Boote* half-flotilla, with an enlarged crew of twenty-five men. The "S-1" was sold on 10 December 1936 to the Spanish Navy and become the *Badajoz*.

Schnellboote "S-26"

The "S-26" in March, 1941. The boat was operating with the 1st *S-Boote* flotilla based in IJmuiden (Holland). The "S-26" to "S-29" series was a follow-up to the "S-30" to "S-37". The "S-26" was 35 metres long and driven by three 2,000-hp 20-cylinder Mercedes Benz MB 501 diesel engines, giving it a maximum speed of 39.9 knots and a 700-mile radius of action. The main armament was composed of two 533-mm torpedo launching tubes with four G7-type torpedoes. A 20-mm rapid-fire cannon was placed in the rear. The prow of the boat was equipped with a 7.92mm MG 34 machine gun. Smoke pots completed the defensive equipment. Six EMC-type anti-ship contact mines were attached to the stern.

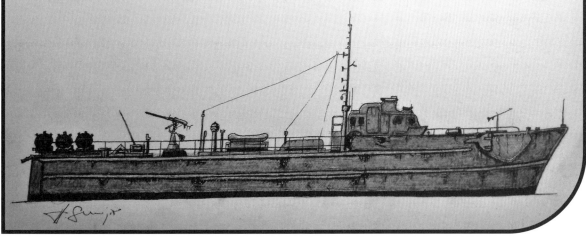

Schnellboote "S-701"

The "S-701" in April, 1945. This torpedo boat was part of the 8th *S-boote* flotilla. It had been delivered to the *Schnellbootwaffe* in July, 1944, by the company Danziger Waggon-Fabrik which built the "S-701"to "S-709"series. The "S-701"was 40 metres long with a 124-ton displacement, and was propelled by three 2,500-hp Mercedes Benz MB 511 engines allowing it to reach a top speed of 44 knots using the *Lürssen Effekt*. Its radius of action at 35 knots was 700 nautical miles. The vessel was armed with two 533-mm torpedo tubes, capable of launching four G7es T5 Zaunkönig torpedoes with acoustic heads, as well as traditional torpedoes. Secondary weapons included a 40-mm Bofors Flak 28 cannon in the rear, the double 20-mm Flak 38 turret in the centre and 20-mm Flak 38 piece in the low firing dugout up front. Radar equipment included a FUMB antenna, a FUMB 10 Borkum radar and a FUMO 62 Hohentwiel radar. The crew was made up of two officers and twenty-eight men.

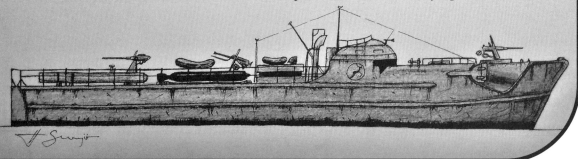

Chapter 1

Introduction

Before the war of 1939-1945 once again divided Europe, the German Navy developed new weapons that would be used on all battlefields until the the fall of the Third Reich. As well as the reconstruction of the German Navy, the first *Schnellboote* (or *S-Boot,* meaning "fast boat") were built. The *Schnellbootwaffe* (a branch of the *Kriegsmarine*, including their command structure and warfare potential) was created in the early 1930s, at the same time as the regenerated *Kriegsmarine*. Young officers, most of whom learned their craft in the old Imperial Navy, would take responsibility for the operational use of these revolutionary vessels, which boasted superior nautical performances and characteristics at the time.

Working with the naval engineers of Lürssen Shipyard, a company founded over fifty years before not far from Bremen, the Germans designed combat weapons never surpassed by their opponents. After the first series of *Schnellboote* were launched into the sea, constantly improved versions of these vessels would follow in the following years. The *Schnellbootwaffe* would achieve significant victories for the *Kriegsmarine* at the beginning of the Second World War by using these vessels in high-level strategies, including a style of guerrilla warfare.

The British often call German torpedo boats E-boats (E for 'Enemy'), and these fast vessels posed a real threat not only to coastal trade, but also to the movement of Allied ships after D-Day. Admiral Rudolf Petersen's flotillas remained combat-ready until the very end of the war, even after the balance of power had turned in favour of the Allies.

Allied air bombardment of German torpedo boat bases from 1944 onwards failed to destroy the offensive potential of the *Schnellboote* and their crews. The Allied disaster at Lyme Bay at the end of April 1944 shows how Adolf Hitler's guerrilla war at sea was still a dangerous threat, even at that stage of the Second World War. The Allied invasion plans were not yet evident to the Germans, but Eisenhower learned a great deal from Lyme Bay, and the *Schnellbootwaffe* was still potentially dangerous right until the end of the war.

This book tells the story of these special people, whose pirate spirit and guerilla style of naval-warfare is reminiscent of the more traditional 'pirates' and their way of warfare.

Chapter 2

Precedents and First Actions (1915-1940)

Gottlieb Wilhelm Daimler (1834-1900).

The first internal combustion engine was created by G. Daimler and W. Maybach in 1882, and the first 'motor boats', which preceded torpedo motor boats, appeared at the beginning of the twentieth century. The first fast ships of the German Navy from the First World War were equipped with such propulsion. After this first generation of mechanical engineers, a group of young technicians specializing in marine construction would take over and prove to be true forerunners in the field. Among them was Otto Lürsen, who ran a family company located on the banks of the river Weser (Vegesack), not far from Bremen, which was founded in 1875 by F. Lürsen. He was a true pioneer in the design of small, fast and agile boats and produced technology for civilian and military purposes. In 1911, Otto Lürsen won the *Prix de la Cote d'Azur* and the *Grand Prix des Nations* with an 8-metre-long motorboat travelling at more than 28 knots and propelled by two 102-hp Daimler engines.

2.1. First operations (1914–1918)

During the First World War, it was mainly the British and Italians who were interested in developing motor torpedo boats for operational purposes, while the Germans and Austrians gave such vessels a somewhat minor role. The first operational ships in the Royal Navy appeared in 1916. The boats were 12 metres long and were powered by 250 hp engines. They reached a speed of 33 knots, while their radius

Above left: Wilhelm Maybach (1846-1929).

Above right: Luigi Rizzo (1887-1951).

was 250 km. On deck they carried one torpedo tube (457-mm) and two 7.7 mm double Lewis machine guns. In November 1918, the Royal Navy boasted 88 CMBs (Coastal Motor Boat).

The intention of the British was to attack the German fleet located along the Belgian coast (at Ostend and Zeebrugge) with fast shallow-draft boats. Likewise, the Italians built MAS (*Motoscafi Anti Sommergibili*) anti-submarine motor boats at a Venetian shipyard. On 10 June 1918, Lieutenant Rizzo's MAS-15 sank *Szent István*, an Austrian armoured battleship with a displacement of 21,570 tons.

During the summer of 1916, German engineers built small boats with no pilots that could reach speeds of 30 knots. Loaded with explosives and guided by a wired remote control from the shore, these vessels (FL or *Ferlenke Booten*) were used against the Allied blockade along the Belgian coast, but without success. In January 1917, Lürsen's company, known for its successes in civilian competitions, would build Germany's first fully operational motor boat: an LM (*Luftschiff Motoren*). This was a genuine speed boat which could reach 29 knots thanks to its three Maybach petrol engines. However, following two accidents with these engines, Lürsen's engineers developed a series of diesel engines, which were just as powerful as the petrol ones, only more reliable.

According to the provisions of the armistice signed on 11 November 1918, Germany, among other things, had to hand over its warships to the Allies. Seven months after the surrender of the high seas fleet, the Germans managed to avoid the vigilance of the British and sank five battleships, nine cruisers, forty-six torpedo boats and ten other ships.

2.2. Development between the two world wars

The Treaty of Versailles drastically reduced the tonnage of the German Navy. The number of surface units was limited to six battleships, six cruisers, twelve destroyers and twelve torpedo boats, along with a pair of reserve vessels. The Weimar Republic was not allowed to have submarines, and the tonnage of battleships was reduced to 10,000 tons. Nevertheless, the Allies allowed the *Reichsmarine* to launch a program to build twelve torpedo boats, each displacing 200 tons. The old LM boats were re-armed in 1922 and renamed the *Unterseeboote Zerstörer* (UZ). At that time, the activity of the Lürsen shipyard was not limited to orders from the *Reichsmarine*, and the Vegasack company also built a series of small boats intended for police service on the Rhine. In 1926, the larger boats *Rheinpolizei VI* and *Rheinpolizei VII* were delivered to the police flotilla on the Rhine.

Likewise, Lürsen's company started to export several vessels of varying tonnage for the US Coast Guard. Among them was the *Inishowen*, a vessel whose shape and nautical characteristics were very similar to those of the first series of *S-boote* launched at the beginning of the 1930s. At the time, an American millionaire ordered a magnificent motor yacht, the *Oheka II*, with unique nautical abilities and a speed of 34 knots. This prompted the *Reichsmarine* in 1929 to ask the Lürsen Shipyard to build a prototype high-speed torpedo boat based on that model. After less than a year of operation and testing, the torpedo boat UZ 16 was completed. Its exceptional stability at sea and its performance (at full speed it could reach 34 knots) surpassed all other vessels of this type. On 7 August 1930, the first model marked "S-1" (*Schnellboote 1*) was delivered to the *Reichsmarine*.

Mahogany and metal were the constituent materials from which the "S-1" was built, and its displacement was 47 tons. This 26.8-metre-long torpedo boat was powered by three Daimler-Benz V-12 petrol engines with a total power of 900 hp, meaning it could reach a maximum speed of 34 knots. In addition to this drive, there was also a special 100 hp Maybach engine for "cruising" at lower speeds (6 knots).

As they did not want to violate the Treaty of Versailles, the Germans did not arm the boat, although it was designed to receive two 533 mm torpedo tubes and a 20 mm pursuit gun located in the stern. Auxiliary armaments would later change during the war, as Allied air superiority grew stronger. For example, in 1943, a 37 mm

Early version of the MAS, January 1917.

anti-aircraft gun was mounted on the stern of the "S-100", while a further two or four 20 mm cannons were placed in the middle. The next two 20-mm cannons were on the fold of the boat, as were two or three 7.92-mm machine guns. The torpedoes used on these early boats were identical to those used by German submarines at the beginning of the war (G7A). A reserve pair of torpedoes could be set up for new firing within forty-five seconds. With this offensive weapon, each boat could carry a 500 kg anti-ship mine. These weapons inflicted more losses on the Allies than the German torpedo attacks, and were located at the stern of the *Schnellboote*. During 1931, the *Reichsmarine* ordered four production line models ("S-2" to "S-5"), whose petrol engines had 1,100 hp, which exceeded the speed of the "S-1". Their motorization was changed to accommodate gasoline engines totalling 1,100 hp in excess of 34 knots.

The primary innovation of Lürsen's engineers on these models was the way the rudder was positioned. The main rudder was attached at the stern in the middle of the hull with, on either side, and exactly in line with the screw-propellers, two small rudders. When the vessel was launched at full speed, these two small auxiliary rudders were inclined on a 30° angle toward the exterior, creating a water flow around the screws which diminished the bow-wave. This created the *Lürsen Effect,* which increased the speed of the boat for two or three additional knots. At full speed the *S-Boote* had an autonomy of 400 nautical miles, which increased to 800 miles at a speed of 20 knots. The structure of these vessels consisted of different types of robust and flexible wood, while the keel and hull were made of oak. Eight waterproof compartments were created inside, containing six tanks with a maximum capacity of 7,500 litres of fuel. The outer shell of the hull was made of mahogany and the upper and lower decks and intermediate sections of the boat were of cedar. The twenty-five-member crew of the *Schnellboote*, unlike their fellow submariners, had a living space that could be described as almost comfortable. The twelve bunks on board were used alternatively in shifts.

The *86 F* alongside the battleship *Erzherzog Franz Ferdinand*.

At the end of 1932, a fleet of four torpedo boats was under the command of *Kapitänleutnant* Erich Bey. Their task consisted of providing support to the remaining *Reichsmarine* surface ships. In case of war, the plan was to increase the fleet to eight torpedo boats. When the Nazis took power in Germany in 1933, the country was rearmed. It was assumed that in the event of a war, the main opponent would be France. However, the radius of the German torpedo boats was insufficient for combat against targets along the French coast and then a successful return to their bases.

In 1936, four new *Schnellboote* ("S-6" to "S-9") were ordered from Lürsen's company, to be equipped with three 1,300 hp Man L7 diesel engines. From then on, new boats were ordered regularly. The series of boats from "S-10" to "S-13" and then from "S-14" to "S-25" was extended by 4.50 m to accommodate the new V-16 Daimler-Benz MB 502 diesel engines. This enabled the 92-tons and 35-metre-long boat to have a speed of 38 knots. The "S-10" series had an autonomy of 878 miles at a speed of 20 knots, and the "S-14" could cover 1,000 miles at the same speed.

In 1937, the *Kriegsmarine* had sixteen torpedo boats (two smaller fleets with six vessels, plus two reserve boats for each formation), which was a relatively small force in the event of an outbreak of war. At the end of the year, five torpedo boats were sold to Franco's navy ("S-2" to "S-6").

The following year, German production increased and by the beginning of the outbreak of hostilities, the *Kriegsmarine* employed two *S-Boote* flotillas consisting

Szent István in June 1918 after being hit by an Italian torpedo.

of seventeen boats (ten torpedo boats were still in the production phase). The 1st flotilla was commanded by *Kapitänleutnant* Sturm, and included torpedo boats "S-11", "S-12", "S-18", "S-19", "S-21" and "S-23". The surface ship *Tsingtau* served as a logistical support to this group of boats stationed in Kiel. The 2nd flotilla was stationed in Heliogland, and was commanded by *Kapitänleutnant* Petersen. This formation included torpedo boats "S-9", "S-10", "S-14", "S-15" and "S-17", and the support ship *Tanga*.

One "S-7" ("S-13") torpedo boat. The Chinese navy had three torpedo boats of that class in operational service.

"S-Boote" Design

The "S-Boote" that were built by the Lürsen shipyards were remarkably stable, even in bad weather. To approach their target during night attacks their 100-hp auxiliary engine could propel them almost silently at a speed of 6 knots. The German engineers had not forgotten their experiences with gasoline engines during the First World War, and threw all their weight behind diesel propulsion. In 1935, the Navy adopted the MB 502, a 16-cylinder 1,320-hp Mercedes engine. But it was actually the use of the MB 501, another Mercedes engine, which gave the German rapid fleets the tool they needed to meet the challenge of the coming conflict.

The MB 501 developed 2,000 hp and its twenty cylinders allowed it to easily exceed 40 knots at top speed. The "S-Boote" were given three engines of this type each, bringing their total strength to 6,000 hp. From 1943, the "S-100" series were fitted with the 2,500-hp MB 511, and at the end of the war the Mercedes engineers developed an even more powerful engine, the MB 518, which, with its 3,000 hp, could propel the German torpedo boats at 43,5 knots.

The other factor in the astonishingly successful "S-Boote" conception was the internal structure of the boats, made from different types of wood associated with metal parts. For body parts, the German engineers were able to create lightweight structures made of various types of wood, reinforced with pieces of metal, thus ensuring better protection for the vessel and the crew. After 1943, the command bridge was replaced by an armored cabin, the *Kalottenbrücke*, which was round-shaped and stream-lined to insure better protection for part of the crew. Likewise the gunners fore and aft were well protected inside their low-laying combat stations. The crews of the British MTBs were comparatively more exposed than their Kriegsmarine counterparts when under gunfire, and often sustained heavier losses.

2.3. The *Kriegsmarine's* first victories (1939–1940)

In late August 1939, certain torpedo boats took part in preventing the escape of Polish ships from the port of Danzig (now Gdansk). During the first days of autumn, weather conditions in the North and Baltic Seas did not allow for any major *Schnellboote* action, and a similar situation was repeated during the winter of 1940. Therefore, the *Kriegsmarine* headquarters decided to group the T-Boat (*Torpedomine-Boote*) flotilla together with the two *S-Boote* flotillas under a joint command, which was to reduce the number of new units. The priority for the construction of new German vessels at that time was U-Boote (*Untersee-Boote*, ie submarines).

On the eve of the invasion of Norway in March 1940, the *Kriegsmarine* still had two *S-Boote* flotillas at its disposal, which in the forthcoming German operation in the north had the task of protecting the invasion sites in the event of Royal Navy intervention. As part of 'Group 3' (in the attack on Denmark and Norway, the German navy employed eleven groups of surface ships together with nine groups of submarines), the 1st *S-Boote* flotilla took part in the action to capture Bergen. Just before the attack began, the fleet received new boats, the "S-30" "S-31" and "S-32", which were equipped with the new 1,600-hp Mercedes MB 512 diesel engines.

Until this time, the 2nd *S-Boote* flotilla was assisting 'Group 4' and operated during the conquest of Kristiansand. As the Germans did not have quality smaller ships to unload their troops, they assigned the task of transferring soldiers from larger ships to the mainland to the *Schnellboote*. The British used early versions of LCM for this purpose during the Norwegian campaign. It was not until August 1940, with its preparations for invading Britain, that the *Kriegsmarine* would have cargo boats with a shallow bottom for landing.

On 10 April, Admiral Raeder announced that the first landing operations had been carried out as planned, despite the loss of the cruisers *Blücher* and *Karlsruhe*. However, the presence of the Royal Navy created a real threat to the German invasion forces, so it was decided that *S-Boote* flotillas, along with their support ships, would remain at the locations where the landings were made.

The last participation of *Schnellboote* in the Norwegian campaign took place on 23 April at the entrance to Skagerrak Bay. Three French destroyers had to destroy German anti-submarine ships in a night attack because of the danger they posed to the Royal Navy in the waters of southern Norway. In a brief skirmish about three hours after midnight, torpedoes were fired from several *Schnellboote* at the destroyers *Indomptable* and *Malin*, but the French ships remained undamaged.

Yugoslav torpedo boat "T-3" (1931).

2.4. The French campaign

The 2nd *S-Boote* flotilla was the first to take part in the action in May 1940 after the British submarine HMS *Taku* torpedoed the German destroyer *Möwe* in the North Sea, before it was due to meet with the German battlecruiser *Scharnhorst* to provide an escort to its base. All units of the 2nd *S-Boote* flotilla were sent to help a badly damaged German destroyer. At that time, the flotilla's units were divided into two parts: "S-30", "S-32" and "S-33" were stationed in Wilhelmshaven, while "S-34" and "S-36" were located at Stavanger (Norway).

The British reacted immediately to the presence of German ships in that part of the sea and activated the heavy cruiser HMS *Birmingham,* together with a group of four destroyers. At the same time another group of British ships from the Fifth Destroyer Division, under the command of Captain Lord Louis Mountbatten, was rushing north. Around noon, a third group of destroyers left the port of Scapa Flow in the Orkney Islands.

Mountbatten's group of four destroyers met the cruiser HMS *Birmingham* and her entourage in the late afternoon. Patrolling over the area, *Dornier 18* spotted British warships at 19:00 and alerted units of the 2nd *S-Boote* flotila, which were only 80 nautical miles from the scene. Half an hour later, two destroyers escorted by a British cruiser met with German torpedo boats "S-30", "S-31", "S-32" and "S-33". Heavy fire was exchanged on both sides, but no major damage to the enemy was done in this skirmish.

Austro-Hungarian torpedo boat "T-81". Between 1913 and 1916, three shipbuilding companies supplied the Austro-Hungarian navy with twenty-seven such torpedo boats.

When it got dark, the *Schnellboote* carried out a new attack. Despite heavy fire from the destroyers HMS *Kelly* and *Kandahar*, the German torpedo boat "S-31" managed to fire two torpedoes at British targets from a distance of 750 m at 23:30. The destroyer HMS *Kelly* received a direct hit to boiler room N°1 and the ship suffered extensive damage that affected the upper deck, later taking the crew a full 90 hours to transport the damaged vessel back to England. The naval clash continued and at 01:30, the German torpedo boat "S-33" suffered severe damage caused by fire from a British destroyer. Although the entire bow of the *Schnellboote* was torn off (around 9 metres), and the inner compartments VIII and IX were completely flooded, the boat still managed to return to its base in Wilhelmshaven. The offensive tactics used by the Germans between the two world wars proved valuable: after a group of torpedo boats made a surprise attack and fired their torpedoes, the *Schnellboote* would be quickly withdrawn at full speed and under the protection of a smoke screen.

The German offensive in Western Europe in May 1940 forced the French and British to try to destroy Dutch and Belgian port facilities before they fell into German hands. The task of the British Royal Navy was to place mines around Dutch ports, while the French Navy, with the help of British warships, was to perform the same task around Antwerp, Ostend and Zeebrugge. The operation succeeded only in part because of the action of the *Luftwaffe*, which completely dominated the skies. Allied naval forces managed to reduce the use of the port of Zeebrugge by their actions.

During this period, the 1st and 2nd *S-Boote* flotilla were preparing for their participation in the German offensive in the West from their new base in Borkum, which was not yet fully equipped for operations. On 19 May 1940, *Kriegsmarine* headquarters sent two flotillas from the Nieuwport area with the task of intercepting Allied ships that had begun evacuating their troops from the ports of Calais and Boulogne. During the naval clashes around the Channel port, the twin-engine *Avro-Ansons* of the British Coastal Command attacked *Schnellboote*. Three airplanes simultaneously fired at the German torpedo boat "S-30", and one bomb fell less than 20 m from the vessel.

By directly hitting its torpedo in the middle of a 2,000-ton transport ship on the night of 20-21 May, the German torpedo boat "S-32" sank that vessel near Nieuwport. At dusk the next day, two *S-Boote* flotillas left their bases in Borkum again. The 1st *S-Boote* flotilla was to attack Allied ships near Dunkirk, while the 2nd *S-Boote* flotilla took up positions along the British coast to intercept ships that had begun evacuating troops from French beaches. Thanks to information about the movement of Allied ships obtained by the naval intelligence service, the units of the 1st *S-Boote* flotilla and the torpedo boats "S-21" and "S-23" were ordered to intercept the enemy near Dunkirk. Since the French destroyer *Jaguar* was unaware of the German presence in the sector, it was able to sail slowly through the Channel. Shortly afterwards, the

U-Boot-Zerstörer *UZ-14* 1918.

night was interrupted by the explosion of a torpedo fired from *Schnellboote*. The French destroyer was hit not far from the bridge of the ship, but the vessel was successfuly towed to the French coast and grounded.

As of 24 May, two *S-Boote* flotillas had been operating directly from the Hoek-van-Holland base in the Netherlands, increasing the range of German torpedo boats. Two days later, the Allies launched Operation *Dynamo*, the evacuation of the British Expeditionary Corps from the beaches around Dunkirk. On the night of 29-30 May, the German torpedo boat "S-30" spotted the British destroyer HMS *Wakeful*, returning to England along the Y route. This was one of three routes envisioned by the British Admiralty to evacuate Dunkirk: "Route Z" was the shortest and went from the south side of Dunkirk to Dover. "Route X" passed through the middle, by the embankments of Goodwin Sands, while the longest evacuation route, "Y", went north from Dunkirk to Dover. The German *Schnellboote* fired their two torpedoes from a distance of 600 m, the trail of which was faintly outlined at night. The British ship did not have time to manoeuvre due to the small distance from the attacker, and two

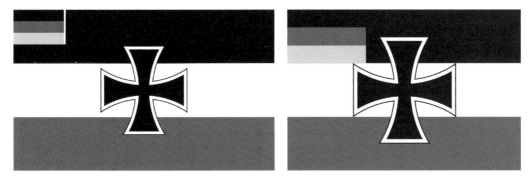

Above left: War flag of the Imperial Navy (1922/23-1933).

Above right: *Gösch* of the Imperial Navy (1922/23-1933).

explosions halved the ship. In just a few minutes the ship sank, dragging down with it several hundred British soldiers who had been evacuated from Dunkirk. At about the same time, the German "S-34" torpedo boat patrolled along the British coast, along with other units of the 2nd *S-Boote* flotilla, where it sank the freighter SS *Aboukir*.

On the last day of May 1940, the *Schnellboote* attacked the *Sirocco* torpedo boat while it was transporting British and French troops to England. Using the night as a shelter, the German torpedo boats "S-26" and "S-23" launched an attack around 01:00. Two torpedoes grazed the bow of the ship and disappeared into the darkness, while almost simultaneously another pair of torpedoes hit the starboard side of the stern. The explosions took away part of the ship's roof, and the engine room was filled with water. Two minutes later the ship capsized on the starboard side and sank, along with 480 soldiers and one part of the crew. Around the same time, a German torpedo boat "S-24" intercepted a *Cyclon* torpedo boat on its way to Calais during a patrol along the British coast. The French boat managed to avoid the first torpedo fired from the *Schnellboot*, but the second underwater projectile tore the bow of the *Cyclone* right next to its 130 mm double cannon. Although the damage was great, the crew of the French boat managed to reach Brest. The 2nd *S-Boote* flotilla continued operations until 1 June. The "S-34" torpedo boat sank the armed trawler *Stella Dorado*, and another vessel of the same type, the *Argyllshire*, suffered the same fate when it was intercepted by the "S-35".

2.5. Germans on the high seas

When the *Kriegsmarine* captured Dutch, Belgian and certain French ports on the Channel, it gained offensive bases from which British maritime traffic would be constantly attacked. All convoys along the north and north-east coast of England were now within reach of German surface ships. The 3rd *S-Boote* flotilla, consisting of torpedo boats "S-1", "S-10", "S-11", "S-12", "S-13" and "S-54", was stationed in Rotterdam on 1 June 1940. Beginning on 6 June, the 1st, 2nd and 3rd *S-Boote* flotillas attacked the British fleet from the ports of southern England without much success. Primary targets were the ships transporting coal from Newcastle-upon-Tyne to the south of England, which amounted to around 40,000 tons every week. The Germans had problems with their G7a magnetic electric torpedoes, which sometimes failed to explode even when they hit an enemy ship. The attacks were repeated on the 9th, 10th, and 11th of the same month, but with the same result.

During the day on 11 June, German torpedo boats "S-30", "S-31", "S-34", "S-35" and "S-1" arrived in Boulogne to operate closer to British ports. The British reacted immediately and attacked *Schnellboote* grouped in Loubet Bay with a group of Blackburn Skuas planes. After this action by the RAF, the Germans decided to pull their torpedo boats back to Rotterdam. They would be returned to the French port on 16 June after Loubet Bay was secured from airstrikes by installing anti-aircraft guns.

After joining that group of *Schnellboote*, during the night of 19-20 June the torpedo boats "S-19" and "S-26" sank the *Roseburn*, a British 3,103 tons displacement freighter, at Cape Dungeness. The weather conditions were excellent for further operations, but at dawn on 22 June, 30 miles from Boulogne, a German torpedo boat "S-32" ran into a mine, probably dropped from a Coastal Command plane a few hours earlier. The blast echoed from the front of the boat, killing seven crew members, including the commander of the *Schnellboot*. On 23 June, a new convoy was spotted south of Cape Dungeness. Five *Schnellboote,* divided into two groups, set off in pursuit. The brand new torpedo boat "S-36", from the composition of the first group, which

included "S-35" and "S-31", successfuly hit the tanker *Albuera* (3,474 tons) with two torpedoes. Meanwhile, the torpedo boat "S-19", which was in the second group together with the "S-26", sank the armed packet boat *Kingsfisher*.

The collapse of the French army in less than four weeks resulted in the signing of an armistice on 25 June 1940. The Germans now took over French ports on the Channel and the Atlantic Ocean. Two days after the armistice was signed, the 1st *S-Boote* flotilla (comprising the "S-20", "S-21", "S-22", "S-25", "S-26", "S-27" and "S-28 "), arrived in the port of Cherbourg with the task of cutting British traffic in the area from the Isle of Wight to the east to the port of Brighton. At the same time, the

Navy helmet badge (*Kriegsmarine*).

port of Boulogne was equipped to receive *Schnellboote*. The 2nd *S-Boote* flotilla (the "S-30", "S-33", "S-36", "S-37", "S-55" and "S-56") was stationed in the Belgian port of Ostend, with the intention of rapid intervention against each convoy along the south-east and east coasts of England. The 3rd *S-Boote* flotilla was anchored in the port of Rotterdam.

During the night of 4-5 July 1940, the OA 178 convoy, which had already been attacked from the air by *Luftwaffe* squadrons, intercepted two groups of *Schnellboote* from the 1st flotilla. The attack was carried out in pairs or *Rotten* (detachments) and the *Schnellboote* naval tactics (*Lauertaktik*, ambush) were as follows: when the fleet commanders established the speed and direction of the convoy, eight or ten *Schnellboote* deployed in the line would be sent into operation. At 20-30 miles from the target, a group of torpedo boats was divided into two groups composed of several pairs (*Rotten*). They then carried out the attack in two parallel lines at full speed. Desiring to be spotted by escort ships as late as possible, the two small flotillas attacked separately from each other at a distance of approximately 3 miles. Within the group, each *Rotten* was kept approximately a mile away from the other two boats involved in the attack. Throughout the operation, the *Schnellboote* maintained contact via VHF radio, and all torpedo boat commanders had to work closely with their neighbouring boat to be as effective as possible. The last part of the process was the most sensitive as the *Schnellboote* had to reduce their speed to 10 knots in order to be able to launch their torpedoes in the best possible conditions. Had the torpedo been ejected at high speed, its trajectory would not have been straight. If two groups managed to fire their torpedoes at the same convoy and at the same time, the chances of destroying enemy targets were higher. What is more, the low profile of the *Schnellboote* and their grey colour made these vessels difficult to spot. Thanks to their speed, if the first attack failed, the *Schnellboote* were able to make a second attempt after the crew re-filled the torpedo tubes. Escort ships of the British Royal Navy initially had great difficulty in attempting to intercept these German vessels moving at speeds of 42 knots, and would have to wait for the delivery of new MTBs and MGBs equipped with high-speed gasoline engines.

Meanwhile, the attack on the OA 178 convoy only partially succeeded. Two British ships *Emcrest* (4,343 tons) and *British Corporal* (6,972 tons) were damaged, while the German torpedo boat "S-19" sank a 6,000-ton cargo ship. This type of operation would continue during the month of July. On the night of 24 July, German torpedo boats "S-19", "S-20", "S-21", "S-25" and "S-27" attacked the CW 8 convoy and sank three merchant ships. A little later, not far from the Isle of Wight, "S-27" sank the French liner *Meknes*. The ship had been sailing fully illuminated and unaccompanied, with 1,100 soldiers on board who were returning home under a truce agreement.

The German war flag as used from 1935-38.

The torpedo hit the back of the ship after which it sank, dragging 374 people down with it. On 7 August, four *Schnellboote* under the command of *Kapitänleutnant* Birinbacher attacked a CW 9 convoy south-west of Cape Dungeness, sinking two merchant ships and a 4,000-ton tanker. With the arrival of the destroyer HMS *Bulldog*, the Germans gave up any further action. After suffering losses in July inflicted by the Germans, the British decided in August to reorganize their coastal convoy system. The number of ships in the convoy was reduced to twelve and protection was further strengthened.

2.6. Mine warfare

After the start of the air battle for Britain, operations by German torpedo boats directed against the convoys would take place with somewhat less intensity, as the 1st *S-Boote* flotilla was employed rescuing German pilots shot down over the Channel. A *Schnellbootwaffe* offensive strategy would follow again in early September. When four *Schnellboote* intercepted the CW 12 convoy on 5 September, five merchant ships were sunk and a sixth ship was badly damaged. On 1 October, the 1st *S-Boote* flotilla left Cherbourg and headed for Rotterdam, before finally moving to Kiel on the 26th of the same month. The 2nd *S-Boote* flotilla, under the command of *Kapitänleutnant* Rudolph Petersen, continued its combat activities. In early July, torpedo boats began laying mines at the entrance to the Thames Bay, and during September, the *Schnellboote* continued with this particular mission, which yielded significant results. Mine-laying operations during the dark were often more effective than torpedo attacks. Faced with the danger posed by the *Schnellbootwaffe* and its offensive attacks to their coastal convoy system in southern England, the British finally decided to react. In two British airstrikes in just a few days over the Belgian port of Ostend and the Dutch port city of Vlissingen, two German torpedo boats were destroyed, while the other five *Schnellboote* were damaged.

In October 1940, the weather over the Channel began to deteriorate, so attacks on convoys were less frequent. Due to the losses suffered during the previous months, the 2nd and 3rd *S-Boote* flotilla had only seven operationally ready torpedo boats. Also, the expected new units had not yet been delivered. In the second half of November, when visibility on stormy seas was reduced to zero, a completely new unit "S-38" was sunk by the action of destroyers HMS *Garth* and HMS *Campbell*.

Weather conditions in December prevented any offensive action by the *Schnellbootwaffe*, and it was not until the end of the month that three flotillas of German torpedo boats set sail. During the night of 23-24 December, reconnaissance by the *Luftwaffe* spotted two convoys (FN 366 and FN 367). After two failed attacks on a 1,600-ton tanker and a small cargo ship, the German torpedo boat "S-28" sank a 2,500-ton transport ship. Then, in the second part of the open sea, the torpedo boat "S-29" sent the Dutch ship *City of Maastricht*, with a displacement of 6,552 tons, under the water. During this operation, a wind of 6 Beaufort and 4-metre waves created significant problems for the relatively small *Schnellboote*. Likewise, the presence of a significant number of British escort ships around the convoy further aggravated the attack by German torpedo boats.

The year 1940 ended successfully for the Germans. The *Schnellbootwaffe* had sunk twenty-six Allied merchant ships with a total tonnage of 49,985 tons. To this number should also be added ten destroyers that were sunk or severely damaged by German torpedo boats.

Following the occupation of French ports on the Channel and the Atlantic Ocean, trade traffic along the south and east coasts of England was seriously threatened as *Schnellboote* now operated from ports closer to British communications. At the end of the year the British were aware of the operational capabilities of their enemies and *Schnellbootwaffe*: they were convinced that the *Kriegsmarine* possessed the considerable strength of fifty units grouped into three operational flotillas. However, in the coming year, the British would be able to increase the balance of power in their favour thanks to their new countermeasures.

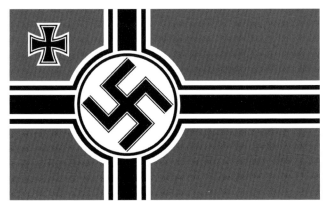 

Above left: The German war flag as used from 1938-45.

Above right: Flag of the Grand Admiral (*Grossadmiral*) and Commander-in-Chief of the Navy in the period from 1939-45.

Chapter 3

The British Response (1941)

In early 1941, the British responded by reorganizing their Royal Navy Coastal Forces and accelerating their new shipbuilding programme. British shipyards such as the British Power Boat Company or Vosper & Company, which had accepted government contracts before Britain declared war on 3 September 1939, had already begun delivering their vessels now deployed to various Royal Navy fleets. The convoys were now accompanied not only by destroyers and corvettes, but also by MTBs (Motor Torpedo Boat) and MGBs (Motor Gun Boat) which were of the same quality as their rivals in the German Navy (*Kriegsmarine*). Applying German tactics, the British began using MTBs and MGBs in joint groups in combined operations aimed at destroying enemy coastal traffic, thus operating through the Straits of Dover (Pas de Calais), the narrowest part (about 32 km) of the English Channel. Together with the new fleet, the British, after the beginning of 1941, developed and used a series of measures designed to eliminate the threat to their maritime traffic, which was primarily damaged by the *Schnellbootwaffe*. The situation began to change when the British introduced squadrons of night airplanes specializing in actions against offshore vessels. During the winter of 1941-42, the Royal Air Force Coastal Command and

"MGB-66" built at the British Power Boat Company near Fort William, Scotland (1942).

"MGB-75" built in the British Power Boat Company (Felixstowe).

the Royal Air Force Fighter Command together launched 187 attacks against *S-Boote* formations, but no German torpedo boats were sunk. German small ships proved to be extremely demanding targets due to their high speed and mobility, as well as their relatively low silhouettes. In June 1942, horrified by such poor results, the British Admiralty (Admiralty or Office of the Admiralty and Marine Affairs) decided to transfer *Fairey Albacore*-type aircrafts equipped with night radars to the Coastal Command. They were joined by two squadrons of obsolete *Fairey Swordfish* aircrafts, all with the intention of carrying out joint actions aimed at searching for and carrying out attacks on German ships.

3.1. *Schnellbootwaffe*

During the winter, British raids became more intense after each attack on the convoys, a fact that significantly hampered the actions of the *S-Boote*. In January 1941, the harsh battles in which the *S-Boote* and their *Schnellbootwaffe* took part could theoretically include forty vessels against England. However, in reality only twenty-one such vessels were operationally ready; the other nineteen were unusable for action because of repairs, maintenance or as part of these vessels were used for training. From May 1940 onwards, the production capacity of the new *S-Boote* was one or two units each month. After November, production had grown to five per month.

   At the beginning of 1941, the rate of German operations was reduced again, primarily due to unfavorable weather conditions. As Henri le Masson pointed out in his book

"MTB" in Romanian service (NMS Viscolul?).

Guérilla sur mer (*Guerrilla Warfare at Sea*), *Oberleutant zur See* Friedrich Karl Künzel, commander of the "S-103", described his troubles as he commanded his vessel:

> *When we left its base in IJmuiden it was -16 °C. This was 28 January 1941. We had received orders to intercept an enemy convoy in the Brown Ridge tun-buoy[1] sector, between Great Yarmouth and West Hartlepool, halfway between IJmuiden and the English coast. The flotilla* [under the command of *Kapitänleutnant* Heinz Bimbacher] *advanced successfully at a speed of 20 knots in calm seas. The moonlight seemed a little indiscreet to us. It was so cold that the sea-splashing drops immediately froze, covering the vessels with a layer of ice from the bow to the stern. Two hours later, the temperature suddenly rose to 0 °C. Just as we were about to make contact with the convoy, we realized that the torpedo tank was all covered with ice on its inside, which meant it was impossible to fire. Then we turned around as quickly as we could from where we came from. When we returned to base, we found the answer to the problem: for some reason the ice in the torpedo tank had failed to melt. We had to use a welding machine to release the torpedo.*

Several operations were performed in February 1941. On 29 February, despite very difficult weather, and as a result of information gathered from two English shipyards,

---

1. To mark the channel that stretched through the shallows, the English used buoys known by the nickname *tuns*. While the Germans were on reconnaissance they managed to spot them, and the *S-Boote* commanders had got into the habit of stopping their vessels near these buoys while waiting for the convoys.

the vessels of the 1st *S-Boote* flotilla took up their positions across the east coast of England. At 01:00, the *S-Boote* located the FN 411 convoy and headed for it. The "S-102", commanded by *Oberleutnant zur See* Werner Toniges, managed to sink the British freighter *Algarve* (1,355 tons). On 26 February three flotillas were deployed across the sea in three groups, and all *S-Boote* flotillas had fifteen torpedo boats at their disposal. At around 21:00, parts of the 2nd *S-Boote* flotilla spotted a convoy rushing north. At the same time, the "S-30", commanded by *Oberleutant zur See* Feldt, noticed the outline of a destroyer about 1,200 metres away. It was identified as a vessel belonging to the Hunt class. Together with the "S-33" next to them, the two German torpedo boats launched an attack on the British ship, using cannons and firing at it with two torpedoes at a distance of 700 metres. HMS *Exmoor* (L61) received a direct hit in the back and was cut in half, disappearing into the sea in just two minutes of chaos. A little further north, the 1st *S-Boote* flotilla found itself in an attack on the FN 417 convoy. At 03:20, the "S-28", under the command of *Oberleutant zur See* Klug, managed to sink a British freighter *Minorca* (1,123 tons).

Torpedo crews and missions

The "S-Boote" in the service of Kriegsmarine had from 24 to 30 people as a crew, depending on the serial type of vessel on which they served. Their missions typically lasted less than 48 hours, as their radius was limited to between 500 and 700 miles. The "S-Boote" bases were located on the Dutch coast and in the southern part of the English Channel, which gave them great proximity to attacks on their targets. During the first two years of the war, missions were carried out during the day, as the Luftwaffe controlled the skies over the Channel and the North Sea. Beginning in late 1941, "S-Boote" fleets embarked on dusk missions, taking advantage of the darkness to bring their vessels closer to their targets and attack without the risk of being intercepted by British aircraft. Switching torpedo boats between ports in Norway, the Netherlands, Belgium and France became standard practice at the time, all with the intention of outwitting British pilots who undertook air reconnaissance.

Before embarking on a mission, torpedo boat commanders held a meeting with the flotilla leader to jointly determine daily targets and agree on tactics to be used during the action. During this time, crews prepared equipment on their vessels: everything had to be well checked one hour before leaving. Diesel engines were extremely important, as the success of the mission and the very survival of the crew depended on their performance. After previous clashes with British escort ships and especially British MTBs, "S-Boote" crews often returned to their bases with only one or two engines in working order.

At sea, sailors had little time to relax. Every part of the ship required successive checks and unwavering attention. Navigation during the night had to be at altitude because there was a huge danger of a collision during the attack on the convoys when the torpedo boats were sailing close to each other and at the highest speeds. Stress and fatigue were present on a daily basis in every German sailor. Standing on a bridge or by deck cannons, at a speed of 30 knots, could be very uncomfortable for sailors because the cold water, which froze quickly, could almost paralyze them.

Encounters with Royal Navy units were usually fatal. Sometimes the boats fought each other at a distance of less than 5 metres, and when a ship ran out of ammunition, it could be driven into an enemy ship to prevent it from trying to escape. Wounds from small or medium calibre guns at that distance were devastating, and crew members who did not receive first aid could die quickly. The men of the Schnellbootwaffe were often exposed to air strikes and mines. Even though their anti-aircraft weapons were successively improved, the torpedo boats attacked by British aircraft did not have much of a chance of escape. When a mine exploded from a torpedo boat hitting it, it was an "all or nothing" game, and everything depended on which part of the ship had been hit and what was destroyed by the explosion.

During the night of 7-8 March, three *S-Boote* flotillas were sent back into action after *Luftwaffe* aircraft spotted a convoy of FN 26 and FN 29 en route to Cromer and Southwold. During that night, the Germans sank seven merchant ships (13,134 tons). The "S-101", commanded by *Oberleutant zur See* Christiansen, sank the freighter *Norman Queen* (957 tons) east of Crowntown. The "S-28", commanded by *Oberleutenant zur See* Klug, sank the freighter *Corduff* (2,345 tons). Under the command of *Oberleutant zur See* Buchting, the "S-27" managed to sink the cargo ship *Rye* (1,049 tons), while the "S-31", under the command of *Oberleutant zur See* Hans Jürgen Meyer, sank the *Kenton* (1,047 tons). The "S-61", commanded by *Oberleutant zur See* Gerner, sank the ship *Boulderpool* (4,805 tons), the "S-102", commanded by *Oberleutant zur See* Werner Toniges, sank the *Togstone* (1,547 tons) while the "S-29", under the command of *Oberleutant zur See* Friedrich Götz von Mirbach, sank the freighter *Dotterel* (1,048 tons).

However, during these battles, the Germans failed to sink any British destroyers, which was incorrectly stated in a bulletin later published by *Kriegsmarine* headquarters. Until mid-April, operations could not be carried out due to bad weather, while the infrequent use of the *S-Boote* was limited to (not particularly harmless) mine-laying, the effect of which also brought benefits to the Germans. Indeed, thanks to mines

Above: "MTB-24" in coastal waters.

Below: "MTB-28" in coastal waters.

"MTB-49" in Portsmouth.

placed on the east coast of England, Allied ships suffered a total loss in 1941 - both sunken and damaged ships - of 230,000 tons.

On 17 April, during a night operation, the vessels of the 2nd *S-Boote* flotilla attacked an FS 64 convoy traveling north-east of Great Yarmouth. Two cargo ships were sunk: the *Effra* (1,446 tons) and the Dutch *Nerens* (1,298 tons), which had transported refugees over to England in June 1940. Meanwhile, the 3rd *S-Boote* flotilla found itself in action near Haisborough Sands, where a convoy was spotted. As the "S-57" and "S-58" began to take up their positions for the attack in pairs (*Rotten*), three British MTBs suddenly appeared, firing with everything at their disposal. The "S-58" received several direct hits in the hull and engine room, but was still able to return safely to base. During these operations, the British showed that they were able to provide a response to German attacks, even if they managed to inflict only minor damage on German vessels. By the end of 1941, naval clashes with much more heavily armed MGB vessels prompted Petersen and his commanders to request further increases in weapons capacity and to strengthen protection on their *S-Boote* vessels.

3.2. The *Kriegsmarine's* new boats

In 1941, the Germans launched a series of vessels on the Western Front, between the Channel and the North Sea, capable of securing their superiority not only in firepower, but also in speed and action radius. The Germans now had the possibility of moving *S-Boote* to a larger number of bases which were strategically far better for *Schnellbootwaffe* than before. Also, a new series of *S-Boote* could reach a speed of 42 knots, while stability at sea allowed them to navigate more efficiently, even under worse weather conditions. With a displacement of 92.5 tons and a length of 34.94 metres, these brand new models ("S-38" to "S-53") could provide the German Navy with a platform for dealing a deadly blow to trade along the coast of Britain until the Allied invasion of Normandy in June 1944.

The torpedo boat "S-38" was equipped with three diesel MB 501 engines, each of which had 2,000 hp, and could maintain a top speed of 44 knots for several minutes. The vessel was armed with two 533 mm calibre torpedo tubes, two 20 mm calibre guns mounted on the bow and stern, and after 1943, a 37 mm calibre Bofors gun. From the end of 1942, the commander's bridge was modified and its entire structure armoured.

German torpedo boats sets sail from the port of Kirkenes, on the Norwegian Arctic coast.

A German patrol boat on the French coast (1942). This type of boat is very similar to the German "S-Boote".

These new German vessels, which successively underwent numerous technological improvements, were able to defy the Allies on all the seas where operations took place during the Second World War.

On 29 April 1941, a new mine-laying operation was launched, offering three *S-Boote* flotillas the opportunity to participate in the work together. The 1st and 2nd *S-Boote* flotillas undertook an operation north of Cromer. At 01:15, HMS *Worcester* and HMS *Costworld*, as part of the 16th Destroyer Fleet, were able to identify the vessels of the 1st *S-Boote* flotilla, but failed to carry out an attack. In a potentially deadly game of hide and seek at sea, which lasted until 04:00, the *S-Boote* managed to discover a convoy of EC 13 with fifty-seven ships. The torpedo boats "S-26" (*Oberleutnant zur See* Fimmen) and "S-29" (*Oberleutnant zur See* von Mirbach) fired torpedoes at three British cargo ships, but only one ended up at the bottom of the sea: *Ambrose Fleming* with 1,555 tons of displacement.

Meanwhile, two torpedo boats of the 3rd *S-Boote* flotilla ("S-61" and "S-58") laid mines in the area between Haisborough Tail and Hammond's Knoll at the mouth of the River Thames. The crews of the German *S-Boote* were surprised when they came across the British vessels MGB-61 and MGB-59, which belonged to the 6th fleet of MGB stationed in Portsmouth. The fierce battle that took place between the *S-Boote*

A German patrol boat closely resembling the "S-Boote." Eight such Dutch boats were confiscated in the Netherlands in 1940. They were reworked and transferred to the service of *Kriegsmarine*, only to be transferred to the Mediterranean via the European mainland in 1942.

and the MGBs lasted 25 minutes. During the skirmish, the "S-61" fired 800 missiles from its 20 mm cannon without seriously damaging any enemy vessel. Together with the conflict of 17 April that same year, this was the second direct conflict between German and British coastal forces.

By the end of May, three German fleets were leaving the western sector of the front and heading for the port of Swinemünde to reorganize and prepare for Operation *Barbarossa*.

The following is a report from the ship's logbook by *Oberleutnant zur See* Hans Weber, commander of the torpedo boat "S-35" (part of the 3rd *S-Boote* flotilla) on 19 May 1941:

In the evening of 18 May, the weather finally began to improve. There was no sailing for two whole weeks because it was bad; we were all very anxious about not going into action. 10:00 a.m. meeting with flotilla commander, departure scheduled for 9:00 p.m. Five vessels have to participate in the operations, and we will all meet with two other units belonging to the Petesen's flotilla, which will join us in our contact zone.

It is a routine mission, one we have completed many times: laying mines along the coast of Britain or at the mouth of the River Thames. Until recently the English did not react to our nightly actions, but in the last two months their coastal forces became more aggressive and we were forced to respond to their attacks. Each torpedo boat could carry three mines (EMC-type), which seem to have caused our neighbors on the other side of the Channel serious concerns. Laying mines takes a toll on the lives of many people and the loss of materials, all with the damage they do to surface ships.

The weather has calmed down, and we are approaching the enemy shore at a reduced speed; it is now between 22:00 and 23:00, the wind arrives and the sea becomes more and more demanding to drive. The calm did not last long. We now have three-metre waves and good force thanks to the wind blowing at us from behind: our target is still far away. Wagner's 'S-54' lost two mines due to cable breakage; our crew is at the stern where they check the cables to which the EMC mines are attached. They seem to keep them well attached.

The weather is against us now and it is getting worse in the next hour. It is 1:30 and an order arrives for all vessels to change the direction of navigation. Return to base.

On 1 June 1941, the 4th flotilla ("S-19", "S-20", "S-22", "S-24" and "S-25") arrived in Rotterdam and a month later, two new vessels were added to this flotilla: "S-107" and "S-49" (the "S-63" arrived in October of that year).

A new conflict took place between the *S-Boote* and the MGBs of the 6th Fleet during the night hours of 20-21 June, when the *S-Boote*'s mine-laying missions were in process. Three MGBs ("58", "59" and "65") managed to surprise "S-20", "S-22"

"S-9", 1933.

An unidentified "*S-Boot*" ("26" or "38") with a shielded bridge for protection against air strikes.

and "S-24", and carried out an attack from a distance of 1,500 and 600 metres. German crews responded by firing their 20 mm cannons and their MG-34 machine guns without damaging enemy vessels, whose crews stopped fighting after a few minutes.

On 24 June 1941, the *S-Boote* flotilla left the North Sea for Cherbourg. Over the next two months, most missions involved laying mines at night near the Isle of Wight and the Portland Peninsula. Only one ship was sunk during that period, on 11 August 1941. The operation was carried out by the crew of the "S-4", commanded by *Leutnant zur See* Max Günther, who managed to sink the Sir Russell (1,548 tons). As usually happened, during this attack the timely arrival of British destroyers managed to prevent other *S-Boote* from further actions aimed at destroying the convoy. In early October 1941, the 2nd *S-Boote* flotilla ("S-41", "S-47", "S-53", "S-62" and "S-105"), with the exception of four torpedo boats, was sent to the Western Front. They were "S-42", "S-44", "S-45" and "S-46", which were sent to the Arctic Sea with the aim of protecting German ships operating near Nordkapp, the area where there was strong Soviet naval activity. These vessels would form the backbone from which the future 8th *S-Boote* flotilla would be formed.

Left: Daimler Benz diesel engine type MB 518/3.

Below: A British *Fairey Albacore* aircraft during flight.

3.3. The raids continue

The actions of the *Schnellbootwaffe* on the Western Front continued. During the night of 19-20 November 1941, the 2nd and 4th *S-Boote* flotillas set out on a mission to intercept a large convoy spotted near buoy 56. At 00:20, several British freighters appeared at the entrance to the Channel. The Germans reacted quickly and rushed towards the vessels, which had no escort ship. The torpedo boat "S-105" (*Leutnant zur See* Howaldt) managed to sink the steamer *Aruba* (1,159 tons), while the "S-41" (*Oberleutnant zur See* Paul Popp) sent a *Waldinge* freighter of 2,462 tons of displacement to the bottom of the sea. Tanker *War Mehtar,* with a displacement of 5,502 tons, became the target of the torpedo boat "S-104" (*Oberleutnant zur See* Rebensburg), and the power of the blow halved the ship thanks to a direct hit by a torpedo that turned it into a fireball at sea.

British aircraft *Fairey Swordfish Mk I* armed with a torpedo, 1940.

At the same time, the second group of S-Boote took up their positions at the entrance to the Channel where buoy 54 was located, waiting for the second convoy. However, the timely arrival of British destroyers forced the German torpedo boats to leave the battlefield. When the first group of S-Boote finished their attack near buoy 56, which was not far from the area of buoy 54, they left the area at high speed and tried at all costs to avoid any encounters with enemy destroyers. Suddenly, the commander of the "S-62" torpedo boat, *Oberleutnant zur See* Hermann Opdenhoff, most likely due to a misunderstanding while receiving orders, turned sharply to the starboard side of the ship. The "S-47" torpedo boat, travelling beside it, was forced to change direction to avoid a collision. As it abruptly changed course, the "S-47" suddenly found itself in front of the "S-41", which was speeding along behind the "S-62" and "S-47". Following a collision, the "S-41" suffered great damage and water began to fill the engine room, with the crew working hard to keep the boat afloat. The torpedo boat "S-47" did not suffer any serious damage, and the vessel was towed away by the "S-62". All were under the protection of the torpedo boat "S-104", and all three vessels, at low speed, tried to find their way safely back to the Rotterdam base.

Before this, having been informed of the accident, the torpedo boats "S-53" and "S-105" had set out with the aim of rescuing the "S-41". The moment the British learned of the German attack, they quickly sent four MGBs from the 6th Fleet under the orders of Lieutenant Commander Hichens.

Nicknamed "Hitch", he had been born in Cornwall in 1909 and had been attracted to the seas from an early age. In 1941 he was 32 years old and a member of the Royal Naval Volunteer Reserve. He is one of the ones deserving the most

"MGB-314" (14th fleet of "MGB").

credit for devising the idea of combining MTBs and MGBs in operations against the Germans. Thanks to him, the British, after their first duels with the *S-Boote*, significantly modernized the armament of their MGBs. He earned two British DSO (Distinguished Service Order) and three British DSC (Distinguished Service Cross) medals, but was tragically killed in action on 13 April 1943, after participating in 148 missions and 14 naval skirmishes. In 1944, his book *We Fought them in Gunboats*, in which he recalled his war experiences, was published posthumously.

On this occasion, two British torpedo boats had to give up due to problems with their engines, meaning only the MGB-64 (Lieutenant Commander Hichens) and MGB-67 (Lieutenant G.R. Campbell) were able to attack the Germans who were in retreat. West of the Hook of Holland, Commander Hichens suddenly spotted a group of three German torpedo boats with their engines stopped. Since they did not respond to the reconnaissance signals sent to them, the British decided to attack the *S-Boote* group. At a distance of 300 metres, the MGBs attacked the Germans at full speed using all of the weapons at their disposal. The Germans, however, managed to find their way through and take up positions to respond to the British MGB attack. They attacked each other three times, in parallel lines, all accompanied by gunfire that evoked memories of the old clashes of European sailing ships that fought in relentless duels. Only the torpedo boat "S-62" managed to fire 600 20 mm shells. The British MGB-64 was hit, and its 20 mm *Oerlikon* cannon was destroyed in the explosion. Luckily, the MGB-63 fared much better, almost without damage. Therefore, the Germans decided to withdraw, leaving behind the "S-41", which was pierced with holes through which water was pouring in. Its crew was picked up by the torpedo boats "S-53" and "S-105".

As Hichens headed back for Britain, he spotted the silhouette of the "S-41" torpedo boat, almost submerged, and barely floating in the sea. Once the British were convinced that the Germans had not designed a trap for them, they decided to switch to a German vessel with a few sailors. However, they were not able to tow the German torpedo boat with them, and a little later the "S-41" sank.

At the end of November 1941, units of the 4th *S-Boote* flotilla launched numerous and successful attacks around the area of buoys 55A and 56. On the night of 23 November 1941, the torpedo boat "S-109" (*Leutnant zur See* Bosse) managed to sink the tanker *Virgilia*, and the crew of "S-51" (*Oberleutnant zur See* Günter Jürgenmeyer) did the same to the British freighter *Blairnevis* (4,155 tons of displacement). During these battles, the torpedo boat "S-52" (*Oberleutnant zur See* Karl Müller) also managed to send the Dutch steamer *Groenlo*, with a total displacement of 1,984 tons, to the bottom of the sea. On 28 November 1941, the torpedo boats "S-64", "S-50", "S-51" and "S-52" were en route not far from buoy 58, north of Cromer, where they set the trap for the convoy. The crew of the

"MGB-328" and "MGB-330", near Dover.

torpedo boat "S-51" carried out an attack and sank the ship *Cormash* (2,848 tons) after they failed to attack a tanker of 7,000 tons of displacement. At the same time, from a distance of 1,500 metres, the crew of the "S-52" sent the British freighter *Empire*, with 2,840 tons of displacement, to the bottom.

The *Schnellbootwaffe* continued its actions during early December 1941 as the vessels of the 2nd *S-Boote* flotilla carried out a mine-laying mission in the areas around buoys 54B and 57, east of Orford Ness. In the period from 2-25 December 1941, the Germans destroyed twelve merchant ships thanks to these mines, with a total tonnage of destroyed Allied ships measuring 50,396 tons. The German results for 1941 were more than satisfactory. The *Schnellbootwaffe* managed to sink twenty-nine merchant ships with a total tonnage of 58,854 tons, which does not include vessels that were damaged or sunk due to mines.

"MGB-316" at full speed.

"MGB-316" at rest.

A brand new model of German torpedo boats, type "S-38" and "S-100", began to come off the production line, with improved torpedo tubes and new 20 mm cannons. These guns had a higher projectile firing speed and could be used for combat at sea or as anti-aircraft weapons. The British, on the other hand, were fully aware of the threats to their trade routes by German *S-Boote* raids, and decided to make an unprecedented effort to increase their coastal forces. In 1941 twenty-four 14-ton MGB Fairmile Type C boats were delivered to the Royal Navy (MGBs "312" to "335"). They were armed with a 37 mm cannon, and could reach a speed of 25 knots. At the beginning of 1942, they were able to count seven fleets filled with MTB boats, nine fleets with MGB vessels and eighteen fleets filled with ML-type vessels, all of which were deployed throughout the North Sea or in the English Channel. In that same combat zone, the Germans had only twelve operationally ready torpedo boats. The 1st *S-Boote* flotilla was under repair in Kiel, while the 2nd *S-Boote* flotilla had four vessels, plus one extra vessel from the 1st flotilla, which had its base in Rotterdam. The 4th *S-Boote* flotilla had six operationally ready vessels, which were also based in Rotterdam. The 6th *S-Boote* flotilla had only one operationally ready boat, also in Rotterdam.

"MGB-061".

Chapter 4

The Mediterranean (1941–45)

On the eve of 7 October 1941, the "S-31", "S-33", "S-34", "S-35" and "S-61" left the base in Wilhelmshaven and headed for Rotterdam. This first group of *S-Boote* from the 3rd flotilla headed to the Mediterranean in order to provide support to Italian vessels of the Italian Navy (*Regia Marina*) operating from Tripolitania. The Italians were experiencing increasing problems with ships of the British Royal Navy, while on land, the military situation for the Italian expeditionary corps was becoming extremely alarming.

View of the port of La Spezia (nineteenth century).

Valletta, the capital of Malta.

Twelve torpedo boats along the Rhine headed for the city of Manheim and had reached Strasbourg by 14 October 1941. It would take them more than a month to reach Port-Saint-Louis-du-Rhone and the blue waters of the *Mare Nostrum* (the Mediterranean), and during this time the vessels of the 3rd S-Boote flotilla were carefully camouflaged, especially as they crossed the Rhine and Rhône canals, with fake structures being built on their decks to make them look like ordinary tug boats.

On 18 November the vessels sailed into the port of La Spezia, where they spent a week being resupplied. Finally, on 1 December 1941, these torpedo boats sailed into the port of Augusta on the east coast of Sicily, and the port would become their first operational base.

4.1. The blockade of Malta

Their first action in the Mediterranean took place on 12 December 1941, when five torpedo boats laid mines around Malta. Operations against Malta and its port would continue on an almost daily basis throughout December and until February 1942. The result of this led to a situation in which the British ships of the Royal Navy experienced more and more problems in their entry and departure from the island. The Royal Navy had suffered heavy losses in 1941: on 25 November, the submarine *U-331* had sunk the battleship HMS *Barham* and on 13 December, the *U-81* sank the aircraft carrier HMS *Ark Royal*. The day before, 12 December, the *U-557* managed to sink the cruiser HMS *Galatea*, and three days later the cruiser HMS *Neptune* and the destroyer *Kandahar* encountered mines laid by the Italians in the sea near Tripoli. The cruisers HMS *Penelope* and HMS *Aurora* were also damaged. On 19 December, three teams of Italian "frogman" from the 10th MAS torpedo boat fleet, commanded by Lieutenant Luigi Durand de la Penna, managed to sneak into the port of Alexandria and, using underwater explosives, sink the battleships HMS *Queen Elizabeth* and HMS *Valiant*, as well as the tanker *Sagona*. The team that carried out the attack was transferred back by the submarine *Scire*, especially equipped for the action, and commanded by Prince Valerio Boghess.

Despite these losses, not to mention the intense German aerial bombardment, the Royal Navy continued to deliver equipment and other supplies to the island of Malta and its capital once a week.

On 5 February 1942, eight torpedo boats ("S-33", "S-54", "S-57", "S-35", "S-34", "S-59", "S-56" and "S-61") left the port of Augusta and sailed into Porto Empedocle on the south side of Sicily. From this new operational base, the *S-Boote* continued their day-to-day mine-laying missions around Malta and Tripolitania (the region around the port of Tripoli), where a large number of British ships frequently passed, delivering equipment and other supplies to British 8th Army units. On 24 March, off the coast of Malta, the destroyer HMS *Southwold* struck a mine and overturned. On 10 May, the "S-31" was also hit and subsequently sank.

On the morning of 14 June, *Luftwaffe* reconnaissance aircraft discovered the presence of several convoys sailing towards Malta. There were five freighters and a tanker, accompanied by the cruiser HMS *Cairo*, equipped for anti-aircraft combat, nine destroyers and four minesweepers. This force left Gibraltar and sailed into the Mediterranean, to be later joined by two aircraft carriers, HMS *Eagle* and HMS *Argus*, the battleship HMS *Malaya*, the cruisers HMS *Liverpool* and HMS *Charybdis*, and a group of eight destroyers. Operation *Harpoon* had begun. The forces that left Alexandria were equally impressive. Codenamed *Vigorous*, eleven transport ships took part in the operation, protected by twelve destroyers, two minesweepers and four corvettes. When they arrived on the high seas, they were joined by eight cruisers (HMS *Cleopatra*, *Dido*, *Hermione*, *Arethusa*, *Coventry*, *Birmingham*, *Newcastle* and *Euryalus*) and fourteen destroyers. Between 14 and 16 June, British forces would find themselves under intense attack from the Italian Air Force (*Regia Aeronautica*) and

Above: The effects the bombing in Valletta.

Below: Satellite view of Valletta.

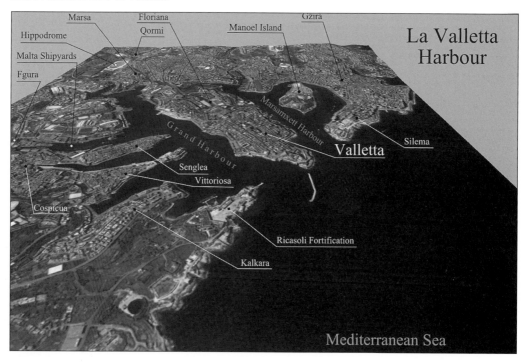

the *Luftwaffe*. The cruiser HMS *Birmingham* and the transport ships *City of Calcutta* (8,063 tons) and *Potaro* (5,410 tons) were hit on several occasions by aircraft from the 10th Flieger Korps. Two cargo ships were sunk: *Buthan* (6,100 tons) and the Dutch steamer *Aagterek* (6,811 tons). Finally, on 11 June, the submarine *U-205* sank the cruiser HMS *Hermione*.

At that time, the 3rd *S-Boote* flotilla was conducting operations from the small Italian island of Pantelleria, located between Sicily and Malta, but also from the port of Derna in Libya (Cyrene). The *S-Boote* were alerted on 16 June to the presence of a convoy, so the "S-36", "S-54", "S-55", "S-56" "S-58", and "S-59" sailed to sea under the command of *Korvettenkapitän* Wupermann, and set out to intercept ships that sailed from Alexandria. The Germans divided their forces into two groups, with the idea of simultaneously cutting and attacking convoys from the north and south. However, the torpedo boats soon discovered that it was extremely difficult for them to cross the defensive barrier created by the forces of the Royal Navy. At each of their attempts, the torpedo boats were overrun by fire from the destroyers.

At 03:00, after several unsuccessful breakthrough attempts, under Wupermann's command, another group of torpedo boats, repeated the attack on the large cruiser HMS *Newcastle*. The "S-56" managed to break through a small crack in the British

Italian bomber *Savoia-Marchetti S.M. 79.*

Italian bombing of Valletta.

defense forces and reach HMS *Newcastle*. From a distance of 400 metres, and despite heavy fire coming from the accompanying ships, the torpedo boat managed to launch its weapon and hit the front of the cruiser. Although hit 15 metres from the bow, the ship still managed to stay on the high seas and be towed back to Alexandria.

The "S-55", from the first group, commanded by *Oberleutnant zur See* Horst Weber, added a new trophy for the German sailors when he torpedoed the destroyer HMS *Hasty* (1,340 tons), which then sank. The convoy sailing from Gibraltar was also going through considerable hardships as it got closer to Malta. Mines that were dumped into the sea the week before by the 3rd *S-Boote* flotilla managed to cause a great deal of damage to the British ships. Three destroyers were sunk: HMS *Matchless* (1,920 tons), HMS *Badsworth* (1,050 tons) and the Polish destroyer *Kujawiak* (1,050 tons); the minesweeper HMS *Hebe* (820 tons) and the transport ship *Orari* (10,350 tons).

HMS *Illustrious* under attack from Ju-87s, Valletta.

An Italian bomber refuelling at a base in Sicily.

Rommel's victories in March 1941 and his rapid breakthrough towards Egypt, after only a few months of fighting, completely reversed the military situation in the North African Theatre of Operations. Tripolitania and Cyrenaica were now under German control, followed by the German siege of Tobruk, where it was now the turn of the British to surrender after a siege lasting 242 days. In less than ten days, the German Afrika Corps (*Afrika Korps*) expanded its area of control all the way to the Egyptian borders. Nearly 36,000 British troops found themselves dependent on supplies now supplied exclusively by sea, and the area in which all this was carried out was no wider than the 48-kilometre perimeter which the Germans endeavoured to restrict even further in the following months.

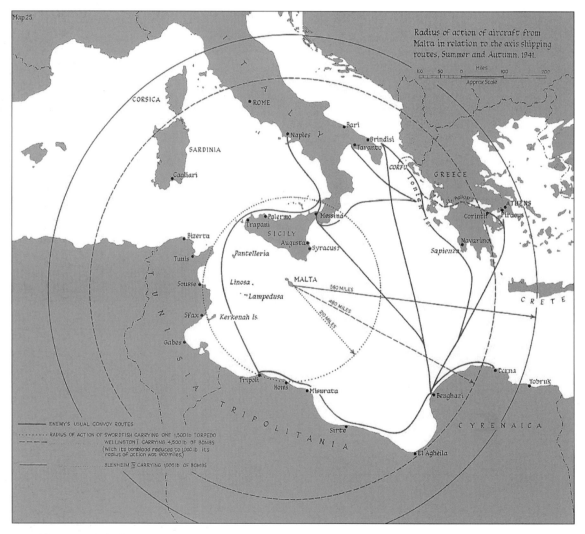

The radius of Allied aircraft in the District of Malta in relation to the Axis Ship Routes (summer and autumn 1941).

4.2. A hopeless situation for British convoys

In line with ground operations, the 3rd *S-Boote* flotilla was mobilized to carry out attacks near Tobruk, in an effort to prevent any British ship from delivering supplies to the besieged garrison. These actions of the 3rd *S-Boote* flotilla included mine-laying missions in the region and the execution of convoy attack missions. On 22 June 1942, the "S-54" and "S-56" managed to sink the steamer *Brook* (1,225 tons). The next day, the "S-36" and "S-55" launched an attack and sent two new British freighters to the bottom of the sea, not far from the besieged city. On 30 June 1942, the Axis forces were only 100 kilometres from Alexandria. On 11 August, a large convoy left Gibraltar and headed for Malta. Operation *Pedestal* had begun. Once again, the British Admiralty decided to mobilize a large number of vessels in order to assist the besieged island. Fourteen merchant ships were accompanied by four cruisers (HMS *Nigeria*, *Kenya*, *Manchester* and *Cairo*, which was equipped for anti-aircraft combat) and eleven destroyers. About halfway through, they were joined by the Force H group, which included two battleships, HMS *Rodney* and HMS *Nelson*, the aircraft carriers HMS *Indomitable*, HMS *Eagle*, HMS *Victorious*, the battlecruiser HMS *Furious,* as well as three cruisers, HMS *Phoebe*, *Sirius* and *Charybdis,* and thirteen destroyers.

Spitfire "Vc" in North Africa. *Spitfire* aircraft arrived in Malta in March 1942.

Operation *Pedestal* (August 1942). View of the convoy under air strikes. The strong air defence provided by escort ships is visible. The battleship HMS *Rodney* can be seen on the left, while on the right is the cruiser HMS *Manchester*.

On 11, 12 and 13 August, German and Italian forces subjected British ships to successive attacks. The submarine *U-73* managed to sink HMS *Eagle*, while Italian bombers attacked HMS *Victorious* and HMS *Indomitable* on several occasions. The cruisers HMS *Cairo*, *Nigeria* and *Kenya* were torpedoed by Italian submarines, and two freighters, the *Empire Hope* (12,688 tons) and *Glenorchy* (8,982 tons) were sunk, in action that was started by *Luftwaffe* aircraft. On 13 August the vessels of the 3rd *S-Boote* flotilla (the "S-30", "S-36" and "S-59"), in cooperation with the Italian torpedo boats MAS, managed to win their share when they attacked ships that had managed to avoid enemy aircraft and submarines. This time the Italian sailors surpassed their German allies from the *Kriegsmarine*. The heavy cruiser HMS *Manchester* was torpedoed by MAS-15, MAS-16 (Corvette Captain Giorgio Manuti) and MAS-22 (Corvette Captain Franco Hezzada). On 12 August the "S-58", "S-59", "S-30" and "S-36" operated in front of Cape Bon (Tunisia). The *S-Boote* operated in conjunction with the MAS-554 (Lieutenant Calcagno) and MAS-557

HMS *Ark Royal* in 1939 with its *Swordfish* aircraft. The ship was sunk by the submarine "U-81" on 14 November 1941 in the Mediterranean.

Operation *Pedestal*, August 1942. The merchant ship *Waimarama* during an explosion caused by a bomb dropped from an aircraft.

(Lieutenant Cafiero) and took part in the attack on the Allied convoys during the night, inflicting heavy casualties, despite heavy fire from British destroyers. Four transport ships were sent to the bottom: *Wairangi* (12,436 tons), *Rochester Castle* (7,795 tons), the American freighter *Alméria Lykes* (7,723 tons) and the *Santa Eliza* (8,379 tons). Five other ships were sunk by *Luftwaffe* aircraft.

On 8 October a brand new 7th *S-Boote* flotilla, initially formed on 1 October 1942 in Swinemünde (Poland), arrived in the Mediterranean. The flotilla was under the command of *Kapitänleutnant* Hans Tumer and by 15 December, all of its vessels (the "S-151", "S-152", "S-153", "S-154", "S-155", "S-156", "S-157", "S-158", "S-159" and "S-166") were operational (from the Port of Augusta). At the same time, the vessels of the 3rd *S-Boote* flotilla were moved to Porto Empedocle, where the fleet was reorganized with the intention of regaining its positions near Malta, and its torpedo boats continued to lay mines at sea and started to attack the Allied convoys. This meant that there were now twenty-two *S-Boote* operationally active in the Mediterranean.

4.3. The retreat to Tunisia

The defeat at El Alamein on 11 November 1942 resulted in the withdrawal of the German Afrika Corps back to Libya, and after the American landing in Algeria (8-16 November 1943), the 3rd *S-Boote* flotilla was forced to leave Cyrenaica in early December that same year and move her vessels to a new base at the port of Ferryville in Tunisia (on Lake Bizerte). This new position allowed the *S-Boote* to simply lay mines at sea across the North African coast and, with much success, to disrupt the movements of American ships that were undertaking essential transport of equipment and other supplies for troops on the African mainland.

The Allies responded by undertaking air bombardments of the Tunisian port. However, these attacks did not result in any great damage to the carefully camouflaged German vessels. The 3rd *S-Boote* flotilla also anticipated operations designed to deliver food to Axis troops fighting the Americans in Tunisia. On 13 December, the "S-33", "S-61", "S-57" and "S-58" left the Trapani base together with the Italian destroyer *Freccia* and the transport ship *Foscolo*, which was transporting oil and ammunition for Tripoli. At around 22:00, a small group of vessels was spotted by a British aircraft and was soon followed by an attack on German and Italian vessels. The *Froscolo* was hit, and the ship turned sideways twenty minutes later. The other ships from that small group then turned back and returned to the port of Trapani.

On 12 March 1943, three torpedo boats from the 3rd *S-Boote* flotilla ("S-55", "S-60" and "S-54") and three from the 7th flotilla ("S-158", "S-156" and "S-157") were tasked with laying mines near the port of Bône. As soon as they arrived

Right: HMS *Victorious*, HMS *Indomitable* and HMS *Eagle*. The latter aircraft carrier was sunk during Operation *Pedestal*.

Below: Map showing the Aegadian Islands, west of Sicily.

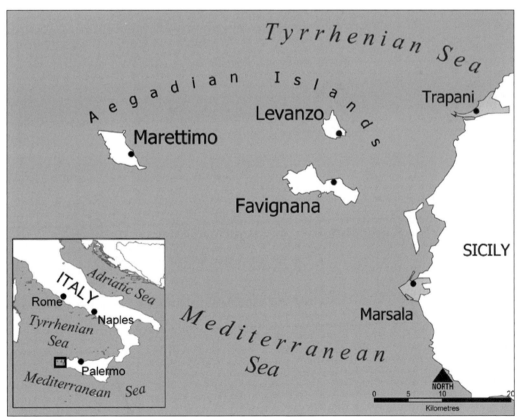

Savoia-Marchetti SM.84 armed with a torpedo.

near the Algerian coast, they were attacked by three destroyers. The "S-55" and "S-60" immediately responded with fire; two German torpedoes were launched at Allied ships from a distance of 1,500 metres. The first explosion occurred a minute and fifteen seconds later; then two seconds later another explosion ensued which illuminated the night. Realizing that the destroyers would soon have them in range, the *S-Boote* dropped the smoke screen and fled the battle zone. HMS *Lightning* (1,920 tons) was sunk during these battles, after literally being cut in half by torpedoes fired from the "S-55", whose crew was under the command of *Oberleutnant zur See* Horst Weber.

Between 16 December 1942 and 12 March 1943, the 3rd *S-Boote* flotilla undertook twenty-two mine-laying operations from the port of Bizerte. But the success of Operation *Torch* had allowed the Allies to take over the installations in excellent condition, which they would then use over the coming months to ship troops and campaign material to Tunisia. By 27 April, American torpedo boats from PT-201 (*Patrol torpedo boat*) to PT-208 arrived in the port of Bône, along with British torpedo boats MTB-265, MTB-316, MTB-317, MTB-61 and MTB-77. At the beginning of May 1943, the Germans found themselves trapped in Tunisia, and on 5 May, as the Allies advanced, *S-Boote* began evacuating people and material to Porto Empedocle. By 7 May the situation for the Axis powers in North Africa had become desperate, and the *S-Boote* were leaving Ferryville for another sea crossing. They evacuated several officers from the headquarters from Tunisia to Sicily, as

The heavily damaged SS *Ohio* enters Valletta, 15 August 1942.

well as almost 100 people and their equipment. After the Axis powers lost Tunisia, the *Schnellbootwaffe* could no longer operate along the North African coast, and all vessels had to retreat to bases in Sicily, while some went to Toulon for repairs. The last actions of the *S-Boote* in which mines were laid at sea near Tunisia would cost

Above: Map showing the borders of the land and sea controlled by throughout the Mediterranean (lines marked with ----) in summer/autumn 1942. Areas under Allied control are marked with dots.

Left: "MAS" of the Italian Navy in the Mediterranean.

the Allies four ships: on 12 May 1943, the British minesweeper HMS *89* (240 tons), on 14 May *M.L. 1,154* (40 tons), on 30 May the minesweeper *Fantoune* (850 tons) and on 3 August the American tanker *Yankee Arrow* (8,046 tons).

4.4. The liberation of Sicily and the landing at Salerno

The Anglo-American landing on the shores of Sicily as part of Operation *Husky* in July 1943 resulted in the overthrow and arrest of Mussolini, and caused severe disruption to the Axis forces. During the operation, the Allies would engage 280 ships, including 2 aircraft carriers, 18 cruisers, 130 destroyers, 6 frigates and a large number of landing ships, while the entire action was supported by 4,000 aircraft.

Despite landing a large force on the island, it took the Allies thirty-eight days to capture Sicily. On 17 August, just days before their withdrawal, the Germans began Operation *Lehrgang*: 101,569 people (39,569 Germans, 62,000 Italians) were evacuated, as well as 9,832 vehicles and 190 tanks, despite incessant airstrikes and the American invasion on 10 August, which aimed to block German and Italian troops in their transfer to the Italian mainland. The Italian Navy had suffered significant losses, especially in transport ships, during the Tripolitania campaign. Therefore, the Germans decided to take over the Italian ships in Tunisia and the French ports, which they controlled. Thus, 128 merchant ships of various sizes ended up in German hands, and it was through them that material and troops were transferred. Many of these ships were then returned to the Italians, who afterwards gave them new names.

The "S-153" and "S-154" from the 7th *S-Boote* flotilla anticipated the evacuation of German troops, and during the night of 16-17 August these German torpedo boats found themselves in combat with the PT-205, PT-215 and PT-216, which was damaged during the battle. The American torpedo boats managed to hit the *S-Boote* several times, but because of their high speed, the American sailors were unable to finish them off. On 24 July, two weeks after the Allied invasion of Sicily, King Victor Emmanuel offered to hand over the government to Marshal Badoglio. Mussolini was arrested and immediately transferred to house arrest on the Aeolian Islands. A few days later he was transferred to a hotel in the Apennine Mountains, where he would later be liberated by German paratroopers as part of the daring Gran Sasso Raid. During the night of 8-9 July, the English and American troops disembarked at Salerno, south of Naples. In response to this move, the Germans occupied Rome. The Allied landing in the southern part of the Italian peninsula allowed them to take over hundreds of ships belonging to the Italian Navy (*Regia Marina*), including five ocean liners, eight cruisers, thirty-three destroyers, twenty escort ships, thirty-nine submarines and sixteen other boats.

After the loss of Sicily, Marshal Badoglio and his troops attempted to take over the *Kriegsmarine* vessels stationed in southern Italian ports. To avoid being captured, several *S-Boote* vessels crossed over into the French port of Toulon. The other *S-Boote* moved to Spain, where they were taken over by the authorities there. The "S-55", on the other hand, managed to break through the Corinth Canal and enter the port of Salamis (Greece), which was still under German control. At the same time, about forty MAS torpedo boats were deployed to *Kriegsmarine* units. Although the British and Americans were far superior in their numbers, German troops nevertheless tried to prevent - or at least hinder - the Allied landings at Salerno.

Above: "MAS" after a military exercise (1942).

Left: Portrait of the Italian inventor Ermann Fiammo (1924). In 1924 he invented a remote control for the "MAS-223" to guard the port of Varignano, with the support of the Italian navy.

On 11 September 1943, the "S-57", "S-151", "S-152" and "S-158" left their base in the port of Civitavecchia and undertook patrols along the Italian coast, searching for Allied transport ships. Around midnight they were able to spot a group of eleven freighters guarding four destroyers, and decided to carry out an attack. The USS *Rowan* managed to detect the *S-Boote* group on its radar and launched an attack at full speed. In just a few seconds, the "S-57" (*Oberleutnant zur* See Günter Erdmann) found itself in a good position to attack and, about 1,800 metres from the target, fired its two torpedoes (G7as) from its barrels. At a speed of more than 44 knots, the torpedoes hit the area of the American ship where the ammunition was stored, creating such an explosion that the ship sank almost immediately.

From November 1943 onwards, the military situation on the Italian mainland battlefield was completely halted for both sides. All twenty-three German divisions led by Marshal Kesselring faced the British and Americans across the Gustav Line, preventing them from making their way to Rome. The Allies were forced to wait five months before their offensive on the Eternal City finally succeeded. On 5 June 1944, Patton and Montgomery's troops, along with the First French Army, staged a parade through the Italian capital.

As early as 1 November 1943, a new *Schnellbootwaffe* unit had been formed in the Aegean Sea, the 24th flotilla, which was equipped with Italian MAS torpedo boats that had been seized by the Germans. These vessels were placed under the command of *Kapitänleutnant* Hans Jürgen Meyer. The torpedo boats had actually been built at Lürsen's shipyards in Vegesack and Bremen, between 1936 and 1938. They were then delivered to the Yugoslav Navy, and the Italians took them over in 1941 after the collapse of Yugoslavia. The vessels included four destroyers, two submarines, six torpedo boats and seven minesweepers.

This flotilla undertook operations throughout the Adriatic Sea from December 1943 onwards. On 14 April 1944, in an American air attack on the port of Montefalcone, "S-622" and "S-624" were sunk, while "S-623" and "S-626" were damaged. Suffice

Torpedo boat "PT-17" of the US Navy. It was built on 12 December 1940, and in April the following year was sold to the British Royal Navy to become "MTB-266".

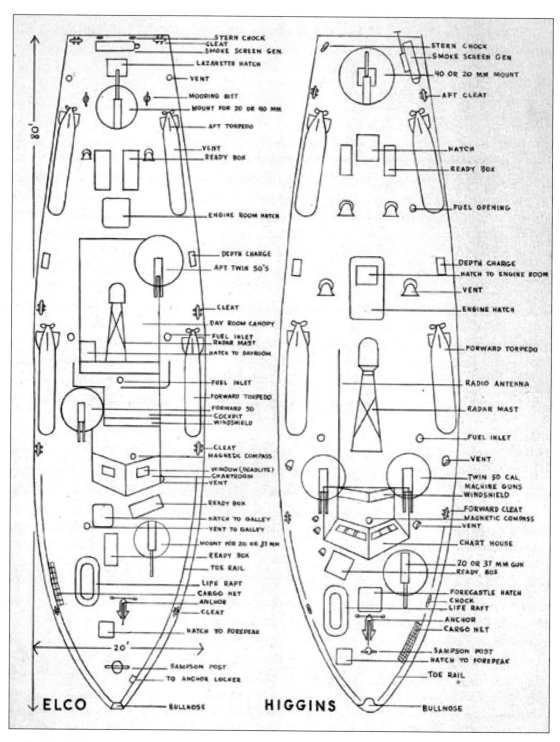

Draft of ELCO and Higgins torpedo boat "PT", published in the US Navy bulletin *Know Your PT Boat* (July 1945).

Ceremony to commission torpedo boats "MTB" at Higgins Industries, New Orleans, on 28 June 1943. The ships present are "PT-281", "PT-277" and " PT-288". Note the standardized camouflage pattern of these boats.

Tanker *Esso Manhattan*. With a specially redesigned deck, it could carry seven motor torpedo boats.

US Navy torpedo boats in the port of La Maddalena, Sardinia.

to say that many battles took place in the Adriatic and Aegean seas right up until May 1945, and of course between units of the Kriegsmarine (including the Italian ships requisitioned by the Germans after the arrest of Mussolini), and the British Royal Navy, which operated out of the Greek islands.

The fighting remained intense, and the Germans were able to reconquer several islands along the Dalmatian coast, which they turned into bases to supply their troops in battle against Tito's guerrilla fighters. During one such operation, on 24 June 1944, the "S-153" (*Oberleutnant zur See* Sven Rutenberg) came under attack by a group of British ships, and was sunk by the combat action of the destroyer HMS *Eggesford* north of the island of Hvar. On 1 September, the three fleets fighting in the Adriatic were reorganized into one larger formation, the 3rd *S-Boote* flotilla, commanded by *Kapitänleutnant* Albert Müller. It was divided into three groups:

- **1st group**: 3rd flotilla under the command of *Oberleutnant zur See* Johannes Backhaus: "S-30", "S-33", "S-36", "S-58", "S-60" and "S-61".
- **2nd group**: 7th flotilla under the command of *Oberleutnant zur See* Hans Georg Buschmann: "S-151", "S-152", "S-154", "S-155", "S-156", "S-157" and "S-158".
- **3rd group**: 24th flotilla under the command of *Oberleutnant zur See* Hermann Bollenhagen: "S-621", "S-623", "S-626", "S-627", "S-628", "S-629" and "S-630".

Between 1 September 1944 and May 1945, units of the 3rd *S-Boote* flotilla laid 2,500 mines at sea along the Albanian, Yugoslav and Italian coasts. This resulted in the sinking of two destroyers, HMS *Aldenham* and HMS *Atherstone*, the minesweeper *Waterwitch* and five MGB torpedo boats ("287", "371", "710", "697" and "705"), ML-558 and MGB-663. At the beginning of 1945, the *Kriegsmarine's* activities in the Mediterranean were reduced mainly to defensive operations in the Aegean Sea and along the Dalmatian coast.

Chapter 5

British Pressure (1942)

The year 1942 would be a turning point in Adolf Hitler's guerrilla warfare at sea. Namely, since the Royal Navy, after managing to withstand the aggressive pace imposed on it by the *Kriegsmarine* over the previous two years, finally managed to take the initiative to its rival at sea. The British had learned their lessons well during their earliest battles in operations against the *S-Boote*, devising and carrying out ways in which they were able to improve the speed and firepower of their torpedo boats. The new MTB types were shipped from production facilities in early 1942, including the Fairmile type D, which could reach speeds of 31 knots thanks to its four 1,250-hp Packard engines. These vessels were equipped with two launch tubes from which

Halifax bombers from 35 Squadron over the port of Brest, 1942.

533-mm calibre torpedoes were fired, while on deck were a 57-mm calibre gun, two 20 mm guns (*Oerlikons*) and 12.7-mm and 7.7-mm calibre two-barrelled machine guns. It was these new models of torpedo boats that proved to be much more reliable than the earlier types of British torpedo boats.

On the German side, operational activities were much calmer during early 1942. Only three new *S-Boote* were delivered each month, which was not enough to replace the lost or damaged vessels. With the opening of new battlefields, *S-Boote* flotillas found themselves scattered in the area from the Baltic Sea, the English Channel, the North Sea and the Mediterranean. For example, in early October 1941, the 3rd *S-Boote* flotilla had left the Baltic in the direction of the Mediterranean, where it had participated in blockade of Malta.

5.1. *Unternehmen Zerberus*

On 15 January, under the command of the Western *Kriegsmarine* Headquarters, the 2nd, 4th and 6th *S-Boote* flotillas were transferred to the ports of IJmuiden, Boulogne and Ostend, all with the intention of participating in a major operation to include other German surface units (around ten destroyers and twenty-seven *S-Boote*).

In 1941, the *Kriegsmarine* General Staff had decided to use its large naval units to carry out an attack on enemy convoys in the Atlantic, while German submarines (*U-Boots*) were already participating in such combat activities. On 22 January and 22 March 1941, the *Scharnhorst* and *Gneisenau* had carried out attacks in which twenty-two enemy vessels with a total tonnage of 115,622 tons were destroyed or captured. In early 1942, these German warships were stationed in the port of Brest, on the French Atlantic coast, where they were joined by the heavy cruiser *Prinz Eugen*. Despite heavy aerial bombardment, the British were unable to sink or at least damage any of these German ships. It was then that Hitler decided to withdraw these ships to Germany, where they would be better protected from RAF air strikes.

According to the plan, the 6th flotilla - with its eight *S-Boote* ("S-18", "S-19", "S-20", "S-22", "S-24", "S-69", "S-71" and "S-101") - was to undertake diversionary raids in the area around Dungeness–Beachy Head, while the 2nd and 4th *S-Boote* flotillas (including the "S-48", "S-49", "S-50", "S-51", "S-52", "S-53", "S-62", "S-64", "S-70", "S-103", "S-104", "S-105", "S-107", "S-108", "S-109", "S-110" and "S-111") were to assist German destroyers in escorting the large surface ships.

At 11.30 on 11 February, under the protection of thick fog, Operation *Cerberus* began as the German ships passed through a canal near Brest (Goulet de Brest) 3 km long and 1.8 km wide, without being detected by a British submarine. HMS *Sealion* had been patrolling the area for several days, but without any success in discovering the enemy. The next day, in the late hours of the morning, a British reconnaissance

Bristol Beaufort torpedo-bomber from 217 RAF Squadron (Coastal Command).

aircraft finally spotted the *Kriegsmarine* ships near Le Touquet (in northern France), which were escorted by the 2nd and 4th *S-Boote* flotilla, plus several more destroyers that had just joined them. At the beginning of the operation, the units of the 4th *S-Boote* flotilla were divided into two groups. The "S-64" came under attack by a *Spitfire* aircraft, after which it was damaged and so returned to Boulogne. On the morning of 12 February, seven *Swordfish* (825th Naval Squadron) aircraft, armed with torpedoes, unsuccessfully attacked another group of *S-Boote*. During the combat, the "S-64" shot down one British aircraft. The British air strikes were largely unsuccessful thanks to the particularly effective support of *Luftwaffe* aircraft. Twenty *ME-109* and *FW-190* aircrafts were constantly flying in the skies above the sea where German warships were sailing. The other 250 German aircraft were on full alert at French, Belgian, Dutch and German airports, providing continuous air support over the sea route by which German ships were to make a bold breakthrough. Five MTBs (MTB-221, MTB-219, MTB-45, MTB-44 and MTB-48) then left Dover to try to carry out their mission to intercept German ships. As they approached their opponents, the British soon realized that they were unable to break through the protective wall of fire from German destroyers and the *S-Boote*, and it was impossible for them to get within 2,000 m of the German warships. Nevertheless, the MTBs fired their torpedoes, but without much success. Some time later, a group of British destroyers

Satellite photograph of the western part of the English Channel, between south-west England and north-west France.

from the 16th and 21st fleets tried to somehow break through the German convoy, but a strong volley of fire from the 280 mm guns on the German warships kept them at a distance. At 03.30 on 12 February, not far from where the Scheldt River reaches the North Sea, the *Scharnhorst* stumbled upon a mine causing it to stop for about an hour to make urgent repairs. At sunset, the *Gneisenau* also ran into a mine near the island of Terschelling. Then at 22:30, the *Scharnhorst* struck a mine again, and this time the ship was flooded with 1,000 tons of water. The following day, the three German surface ships sailed safely into the port of Wilhelmshaven.

One week after Operation *Cerberus*, the 2nd and 4th *S-Boote* flotillas again took part in mine-laying operations and convoy attacks. During the night of 19 February, the 2nd *S-Boote* flotilla attempted to intercept the FS 29 convoy, which was carrying thirty-one ships, all of which were traveling south of buoy 55B. As usual, the torpedo boats were divided into two assault groups heading for their targets in two parallel lines. The "S-70" and "S-105" were the first to fire their deadly torpedoes at the merchant ships, but the British sailors reacted immediately and sent two Hunt-class destroyers - assisted by two HMS *Motor Launch* Ships (type Fairmile B) and two MGBs - which together responded with all their firepower. The fire from the British ships proved to be too much of a challenge for the German sailors, who were on the vessels assigned to these two groups of *S-Boote*. Consequently, they turned carefully and disappeared into the darkness at full speed. The nighttime conditions contributed to situation in which the "S-39" and "S-53" collided. The "S-53" suffered serious damage and water soon broke into the engine room. However, despite serious damage, the "S-39" managed to return safely to its base at IJmuiden. As the destroyer HMS *Holderness* approached the crash site, intending to capture the German crew of the "S-53", *Oberleutnant zur* See Peter Block remained on his vessel after his crew had earlier been transferred to a British ship. Block managed to sink his boat, thus sacrificing own life in an action that prevented the enemy from capturing the "S-53".

Bad weather influenced the German decision to cancel several planned missions during the first ten days of March 1942. On 10 March, the "S-70" managed to sink the British merchant ship *Horse Ferry* (951 tons). The crew of the "S-105" took part in a fierce battle against the destroyer HMS *Whitshed*, believing that they had hit it with a torpedo when in fact the British ship had actually run into a German mine that had been laid several days earlier near buoy 55B by units of the German flotilla.

5.2. Guerrilla warfare in the English Channel

During the night of 14-15 March, the sailors of the 2nd *S-Boote* flotilla found themselves in action, once again deployed in two groups: "S-105", "S-70", "S-111", "S-62", "S-104", "S-29" and "S-108". The German sailors set out for the British convoy FN 55, in which forty-one merchant ships were sailing, whose radio communication had been interecpted by one of the *Kriegsmarine's* radio communications services somewhere near buoy 37. The weather, as was usually the case at that time of year, was very bad: a light to moderate wind (3-4 Beaufort) blew - which raised the waves - and it rained on a night that was as black as ink, thus making it impossible for the sailors of both warring parties to see anything beyond 150 m.

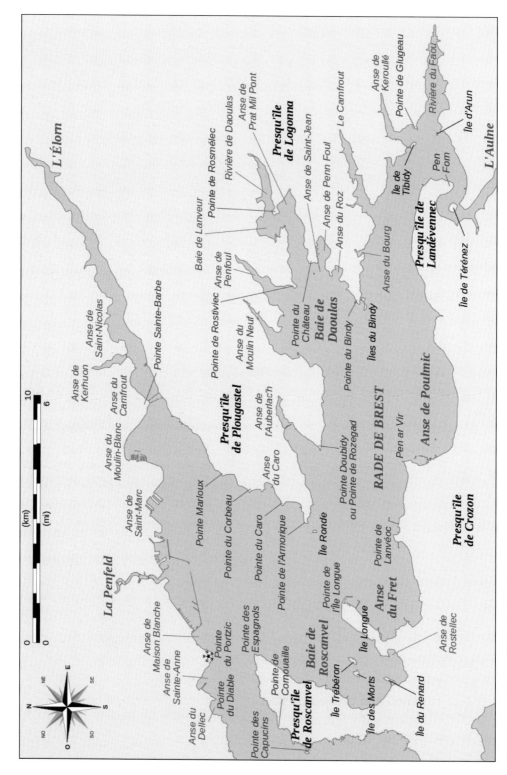

The bay near Brest (Rade de Brest).

At 02:50, crew members of the "S-104" and "S-62" were able to spot merchant ships and destroyers. *Oberleutnant zur See* Roeder commanded the crew of the "S-104", whose direction of navigation, in relation to a British warship, put the German sailors in a favorable position to fire their torpedoes. Immediately, two torpedoes were fired from the *S-Boote* and they soon hit the destroyer HMS *Vortigern* in the stern area. The British ship ended up at the bottom of the sea after just a few minutes of agony. When the British realized that this was a German attack by torpedo boats, they immediately sent in the MGB-87, MGB-88 and MGB-91, which belonged to the 7th fleet of MGBs stationed in Lowestoft. The British sailors quickly headed towards the Dutch coast, hoping to be able to intercept enemy torpedo boats as they returned to base. They were lucky, as around 07:30, after getting lost in the fog, they noticed that the crew of the "S-111" was dangerously close to the Dutch coast. Thus, the "S-111", whose crew was taken completely by surprise, came across three MGBs which immediately opened fire at a short distance from their opponent. The fierce battle, in which the German sailors were overpowered by stronger fire, lasted a very short time, and they surrendered to their attackers. The British sailors immediately transferred the captured German sailors to their vessels, while part of the crew from the MGBs switched to a German boat and hoisted the flag of the Homeland Fleet. Having boarded the *S-Boote*, British sailors collected nautical charts showing German operational zones in the Channel and transferred German weapons from the "S-111" at around 11:00. After that the British sailors hooked the "S-111" and began to tow it, while the MGBs turned in the direction of their Lowestoft base. After only a few miles, they were discovered by German sailors on the "S-104", "S-62" and "S-29", who a few hours earlier had sailed out to find their comrades on the "S-111". After a short naval duel, the British sailors gave up the fight and abandoned their prey when the MGB-91 was hit by several missiles fired from 20-mm cannons. The German sailors then retook the "S-111" and began towing it towards IJmuiden. At around 14:00, the *S-Boote* was attacked by *Spitfire* aircraft, and although German sailors returned fire with strong anti-aircraft guns, they were forced to leave a damaged German torpedo boat, which was soon sunk after being hit by several bombs. Fourteen German sailors were killed in the battle, including their commander, *Oberleutnant zur See* Paul Popp, and his direct subordinate, *Oberleutnant zur See* Friedrich Wilhelm Jopping.

In early March 1942, led by Admiral Hans Bütow, mine-laying operations along the English coast resumed and proved particularly successful. The Royal Navy suffered the loss of three ships with a total displacement of 11,534 tons: on 1 March, the tanker *Audacity* (589 tons), three days later the tanker *Frumention* (6,675 tons) and on 16 March the steamer *Cressdone* (4,270 tons), were sunk after encountering

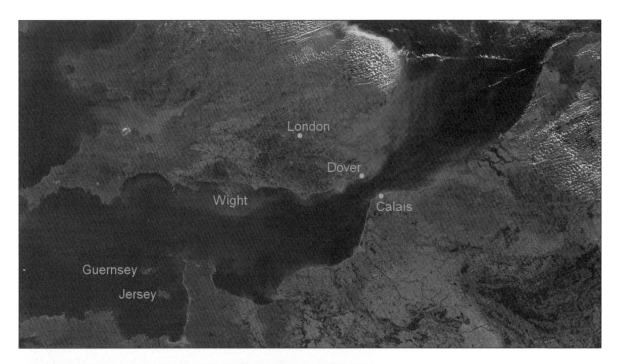

London

Dover

Wight

Calais

Guernsey

Jersey

Above: Satellite image of the English Channel (2002).

Left: Satellite photograph of the Straight of Dover (NASA, 2001).

Above: Cruiser *Prinz Eugen* (May 1945).

Below: Aerial photograph from the first half of 1942. An arrow in the upper right corner indicates the position of the battleship *Scharnhorst*, which was under repair in Kiel after being damaged during Operation *Cerberus*.

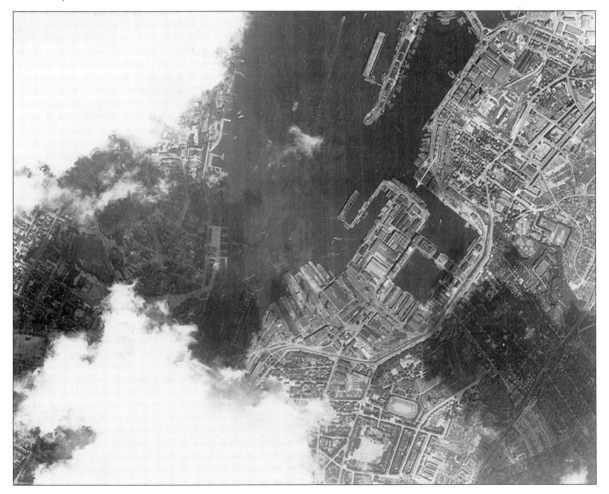

mines. At the same time, two British destroyers were severely damaged after they also struck mines (HMS *Whitshed* and HMS *Cotswold*).

The Allied attack on Saint-Nazaire was launched on 28 March, and the Anglo-Canadian invasion of Dieppe, code-named *Jubilee*, was launched on 19 August that same year. These were both very complex operations, but it is enough to point out on this occasion that their result was, firstly, that the tendrils and the pumping system in the dry dock of Saint-Nazaire were almost successfully destroyed, and, secondly, the Anglo-Canadian forces suffered a disastrous defeat at Dieppe. British coastal forces played a key role in these operations, participating in front lines of attack by escorting larger vessels, and British torpedo boats were part of a designed system of providing firepower to the troops once they were on land. These two extremely complex operations proved to be an incentive for the British to learn how they could send larger forces against German ground targets, while also inflicting heavy losses on the enemy. These experiences would be a prelude and a field test for Allied landing operations in North Africa in November 1942 and in Sicily and southern Italy in July 1943 and beyond.

5.3. The reorganization of the *S-Boote* command structure

On 16 April 1942 a decisive change took place in the organization of the *S-Boote*'s command structure. Until that date, all eight flotillas were under the authority (command) of the Torpedo Boat Leader (*Führer der Torpedoboote*), where the torpedo boats were united by the command decisions of Admiral Hans Bütow. A new command structure had now been devised for the *S-Boote*. It was henceforth commanded by *Kapitän zur See* Rudolf Petersen, who took the title of *Führer der Schnellboote*, a rank he would retain until 1945.

He founded a new headquarters in Scheveningen in the Netherlands and had *carte blanche* (unlimited powers) at his disposal to turn his troops into a deadly weapon for the *Kriegsmarine*. It was he who planned the programmes with shipyards, the development and improvement of armaments and the protection of boats, and devised new combat tactics for his flotillas' commanders. In mid-1942, the *S-Boote* were the only units capable of taking offensive action in the English Channel or the North Sea against Allied convoys. Of all the other *Kriegsmarine* units, except for the *U-Boote*, only the *S-Boote* were able to undertake strategically serious operations. The *Schnellbootwaffe* posed a genuinely serious threat to Allied sea trade routes from one end of the British coast to the other. The capacity and successful tactics of the *Schnellbootwaffe*, in combination with high-level strategy, produced what could be called guerrilla warfare, while their combat performance could only be compared to that achieved by Dönitz's submarines.

Right: Aerial view of Brest. The damage caused by bombs dropped from British planes can be seen around the dry docks where the *Scharnhorst* and *Gneisenau* are located. Not far away is *Prinz Eugen*.

Below: *Halifax* bombers from 35 RAF Squadron undertake the bombing of the German battleships *Scharnhorst* and *Gneisenau* stationed in Brest.

In the early spring of 1942, there were eight operational flotillas equipped with *S-Boote*:

1st *S-Boote* flotilla

under the command of *Kapitänleutnant* Birnbacher: "S-26", "S-27", "S-28", "S-40", "S-72" and "S-102", on the way to the port of Constanţa on the Black Sea.

2nd *S-Boote* flotilla

under the command of *Kapitänleutnant* Feldt: "S-29", "S-39", "S-53", "S-70", "S-103", "S-104", "S-105", "S- 108" and "S-111", stationed in IJmuiden.

3rd *S-Boote* flotilla

under the command of *Kapitänleutnant* Kemnade: "S-30", "S-33", "S-35", "S-36", "S-54", "S-55", "S-56", "S- 57", "S-58", "S-59", "S-60" and "S-61", involved in the fighting in the Mediterranean since July 1941.

4th *S-Boote* flotilla

under the command of *Kapitänleutnant* Niels Bätge: "S-48", "S-49", "S-50", "S-51", "S-52", "S-64", "S-109", "S-110" and "S-107", with a base in the port of Ostend.

5th *S-Boote* flotilla

under the command of *Kapitänleutnant* Bernd Kluge: "S 27", "S-28", "S-29" and "S-45", deployed in northern Norway.

6th *S-Boote* flotilla

under the command of *Kapitänleutnant* Albrecht Obermaier: "S-18", "S-19", "S-20", "S-22", "S-24", "S-69", "S-71" and "S-101", stationed in Kristiansand (Norway).

7th *S-Boote* flotilla

under the command of *Kapitänleutnant* Hans Trummer: "S-151", "S-152", "S-153", "S-154", "S-155", "S-156", "S-157" and "S -158 ", the crews were trained in the port of Swinemünde, and then sent to the Mediterranean in December 1942.

8th *S-Boote* flotilla

under the command of *Kapitänleutnant* Felix Zymalkowski: "S-44", "S-64", "S-66", "S-69", "S-108" and "S-118", with a base in Bergen and then at Bodø.

On 13 May, five *S-Boote* from the 4th flotilla suddenly set sail from the port of Boulogne at 01:00, sailing towards the Strait of Dover in order to meet the pirate ship *Stier* (N° 23) and its escort, consisting of torpedo boats from the 5th *Torpedobootsflottille* and eight R-Boats (*Räumboote* or minesweepers). The British very quickly managed

The *Scharnhorst* (June 1943).

to discover the German formation and sent twelve MTBs and MGBs in order to intercept it. Contact occurred at 03:15. The torpedo ships *Iltis* and *Seeadler* were soon sunk, while the British lost the MTB-220 and MTB-221. The pirate ship *Stier* was forced to set sail for the port of Boulogne at 05:45. The "S-107" crew remained in the combat zone and was able to rescue eighty-three German sailors and three surviving members of the Royal Navy. In the last two weeks of May and the first days of June 1942, the *S-Boote* were used in mine-laying operations in buoy zones 55A and 56, primarily laying LMB and UMB-type mines.

In the late afternoon of 26 June, the "S-78" left Rotterdam and headed for Boulogne. Halfway there, the boat was attacked by several British planes, most likely *Fairey Albacores*. Two German sailors were killed and nine others were wounded, although the "S-78" managed to continue its journey to Boulogne. On 9 July, the 2nd *S-Boote* flotilla ("S-48", "S-50", "S-63", "S-70", "S-104" and "S-109") was again involved in hunting operations. The *Beobachtungsdienst* (B-Dienst), a *Kriegsmarine* intelligence service aimed at intercepting Allied radio communications, provided reports to the *Schnellbootwaffe* headquarters in Wimereux that increased radio contact by Allied ships, namely convoys, had been observed in recent days in the areas around Weymouth and Dartmouth.

Luftwaffe reconnaissance aircraft had also confirmed the presence of activity in several English ports along the coast, and the "S-67", under the command of

Left: The German destroyer "Z-4" leads the battleships *Scharnhorst* and *Gneisenau* through the English Channel during Operation *Cerberus*.

Below: The *Scharnhorst* on its completion of construction.

Kapitänleutnant Zymalkowski, was the first to spot the British ships. The WP 183 convoy was not travelling at a higher speed, probably thinking that it was resistant to danger, and did not have an escort, although it was sailing in a risky area where a wind of 4 Beaufort was blowing. The crew of the "S-67" managed to position their boat so that it was in an ideal position to fire torpedoes from a distance of 800 metres from their targets. Sending its two torpedoes to the 6,766-ton tanker *Pomella*, the ship received a hit and immediately caught fire and sank. Meanwhile, "S-48", "S-109" and

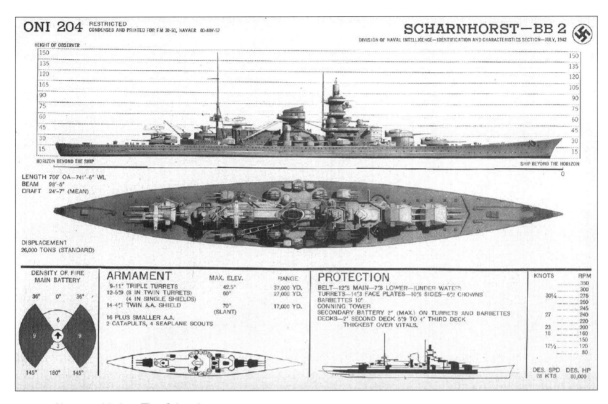

SCHARNHORST—BB 2
DIVISION OF NAVAL INTELLIGENCE—IDENTIFICATION AND CHARACTERISTICS SECTION—JULY, 1942

HEIGHT OF OBSERVER

150	150
135	135
120	120
105	105
90	90
75	75
60	60
45	45
30	30
15	15

HORIZON BEYOND THE SHIP
SHIP BEYOND THE HORIZON
0

LENGTH 766' OA—741'-6" WL
BEAM 98'-5"
DRAFT 24'-7" (MEAN)

DISPLACEMENT
26,000 TONS (STANDARD)

DENSITY OF FIRE
MAIN BATTERY

36° 0° 36°

6
9 9
3

145° 180° 145°

ARMAMENT

	MAX. ELEV.	RANGE
9-11" TRIPLE TURRETS	42.5°	37,000 YD.
12-5.9 (8 IN TWIN TURRETS)	60°	27,000 YD.
(4 IN SINGLE SHIELDS)		
14-4.1 TWIN A.A. SHIELD	70°	17,000 YD.
	(SLANT)	

16 PLUS SMALLER A.A.
2 CATAPULTS, 4 SEAPLANE SCOUTS

PROTECTION

BELT—12'5 MAIN—7.8 LOWER—(UNDER WATER)
TURRETS—14'3 FACE PLATES—10'5 SIDES—6'2 CROWNS
BARBETTES 10'
CONNING TOWER
SECONDARY BATTERY 2" (MAX.) ON TURRETS AND BARBETTES
DECKS—2" SECOND DECK 5'9 TO 4" THIRD DECK
THICKEST OVER VITALS.

KNOTS	RPM
	350
	300
30¼	275
	250
	245
27	240
	220
23	200
18	160
	150
12½	120
	80

DES. SPD DES. HP
28 KTS 80,000

Above and below: The *Scharnhorst*.

"S-70" took action to attack the Norwegian freighters *Kongshang* (1,156 tons), *Rösten* (736 tons) and *Boku* (698 tons). At the same time, the Dutch steamer *Reggestrom* (2,836 tons) was hit by a torpedo fired from the "S-50" and was soon sunk. Finally, the "S-63", which had recently missed the tanker, managed to destroy the armed trawler *Manor* (314 tons). In just a few minutes, the *S-Boote* sank seven Allied vessels for a total of 22,000 tons, without any serious reaction from the British. In mid-July 1942, the first FUMB devices (an acronym for *Funkmessbeobachtungsgerät*, a radio location and observation station) began to be installed on units of the 2nd *S-Boote* flotilla. The device consisted of an antenna capable of detecting metric wavelength radar emissions corresponding to the search range of radars installed on aircraft of the Coastal Command of the Royal Navy. The antenna would start buzzing when it intercepted wave activity at a distance of up to 60 km.

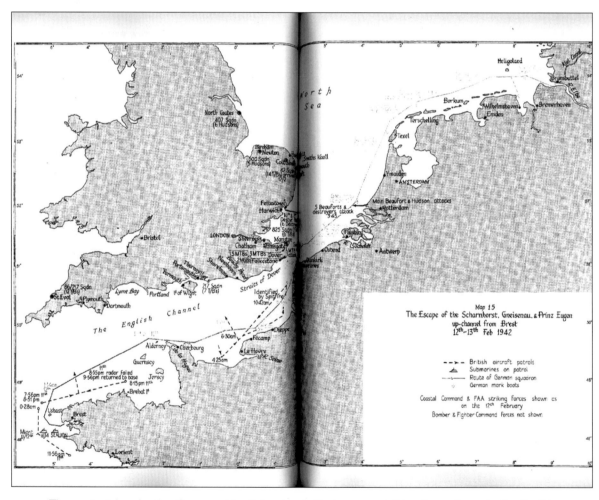

The route taken by the German ships *Scharnhorst*, *Gneisenau* and *Prinz Eugen* through the English Channel, 12-13 February 1942.

On 26 July 1942, the crews of three torpedo boats from the 2nd *S-Boote* flotilla received an order to proceed to Saint Peter Port on the island of Guernsey. On 31 July they met with the crews of the other five torpedo boats from the 5th *S-Boote* flotilla, which had left Rotterdam the day before. On 1 August, six more torpedo boats from the 4th *S-Boote* flotilla arrived in the area around Guernsey, especially around the port. The decision to assemble a group of these half-flotillas temporarily on an island in the English Channel can be explained by the immediate proximity of the British coast and the natural characteristics of the port, which was converted for this type of small vessel. Their attacks would continue during August, and the same ritual would be followed: night attacks against convoys, naval duels with British escort ships, victory bulletins, return to base to load and repair vessels, not to mention mine-laying expeditions sent out from Boulogne, Cherbourg or Saint Peter Port in the sectors around Lyme Bay, although there were also periods of forced inactivity due to bad weather conditions.

5.4. Successful German raids in late 1942

On 1 October 1942, the 5th *S-Boote* flotilla set sail again. As usual, the German torpedo boats operated in pairs (*Rotten*): "S-77" and "S-68", "S-81" and "S-115", "S-112" and "S-65". The crew of the "S112", had recently received a new radar (type Lichenstein) designed to detect targets during an attack. This torpedo boat was the first in the operational service to use this new type of equipment, and as a result, the crew of the "S-112" managed to sink the armed trawler *Lord Stonehaven* (444 tons) near the Eddystone Rocks sector at night. On 6 October, the 6th and 4th *S-Boote* flotillas, along with the "S-63","S-69" and "S-117" approached the Great Yarmouth Sector to intercept a convoy of extreme importance. In less than twenty minutes, the crews of the German torpedo boats managed to sink six merchant ships, as well as one ML, while another was seriously damaged in combat. The Germans, however, suffered no losses during that naval clash. On the night of 13 October, eight torpedo boats from the 5th *S-Boote* flotilla were sent to sea to wait for a convoy in the Eddystone Rocks area. However, the next morning they were ordered to leave their mission and assist in the rescue operation of the sailors from the pirate ship *Komet* (N° 45), which had been attacked a few hours earlier by British torpedo boats below the cape near The Hague (Cap de la Hague). The MTB-236 was the one responsible for the loss of the German pirate ship. Two torpedoes literally blew up the ship, and in that chaos, the *S-Boote* were unable to find or save a single surviving German sailor out of a total of 251 crew members. On 14 October, Petersen's men carried out another successful raid. The 6th *S-Boote* fleet managed to damage two merchant ships, the *Lysland* (1,355 tons) and the *George Balfour* (1,570 tons), right off the coast of England, where no reaction from the Royal Navy followed.

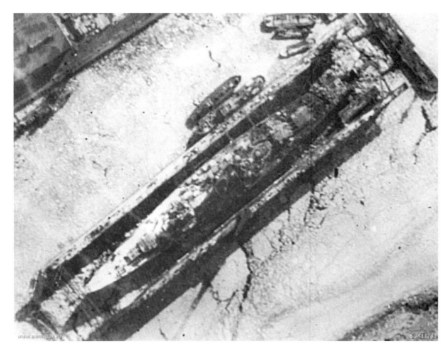

Left: German battleship *Gneisenau* stationed in a dry dock in Kiel, after taking part in an extremely risky action breaking through the English Channel. The action would certainly have been even more dangerous had the Germans not had a strong air force at the time.

Below: The *Gneisenau* (June 1943).

GNEISENAU
Germany - BB
(GNEISENAU Class)
(1939)

In November 1942, further missions continued, in spite of the possibility of being interrupted due to weather conditions, while the *S-Boote* recorded several victories, especially in the southern and eastern parts of the English coast. On 9 November, two Allied vessels were sunk, the Norwegian merchant ship *Fidelio* (1,843 tons) and the British steamship *Wandler* (1,850 tons), and the action was carried out by the crews of the 6th *S-Boote* flotilla. On 19 November, vessels of the 5th *S-Boote* flotilla left Cherbourg together with two combat groups including the "S-82", "S-116", "S-77" and the "S-112", "S-65", "S-115" and "S-81". The two half-flotillas advanced into darkness in accordance with *Lauertaktik* principles. The pairs (*Rotten*) approached the targets while they were separated at a safe distance, so that the British sailors failed to detect their progress until the last moment. Once again, the crew of the "S-112", under the command of *Oberleutnant zur See* Müller, carried out an exceptional operation in which the armed trawler *Ullswater* (555 tons) was sunk. The remaining three Allied vessels - *Lab*, *Yew Forest* and *Birgitte* - also failed to survive as they were destroyed overnight by the deadly pair (*Rotten*) of the "S-77" and "S-116". The total tonnage of the sunken Allied ships was 3,528 tons.

At the end of 1942, the *Schnellbootwaffe* produced more successful actions. On 3 December, the crew of the "S-115" managed to sink the destroyer HMS *Penylan*, which exploded into pieces and sank, along with half of the crew, in less than five minutes. On the night of 12 December, a group from the 2nd and 4th *S-Boote* flotillas sailed from Dutch bases on a mission aimed at carrying out an attack off the east coast of England. The crews of the 2nd *S-Boote* flotilla were unable to detect any enemy ships, but were attacked from a distance of 1,500 metres by a destroyer that fired its 102-mm projectiles. The artillery from the British destroyer failed to hit the extremely fast *S-Boote*, which escaped to a safe zone. The crews of the 4th *S-Boote* flotilla were more fortunate. At 20:15, German torpedo boats intercepted the convoy

"MGB-606" (Fairmile D).

Above and below: British 6-pound cannon (57 mm) with Molins car charger on a torpedo boat Fairmile D.

FN 889, heading straight towards the deadly threat of *S-Boote*. German torpedo boats immediately selected merchant ships as targets, whose crews continued to sail in this direction, unaware of what awaited them in the gloomy light. The battle was short-lived and, as usual, lasted only a few minutes, and the result was in favour of the German crews as it had been many times before. The *S-Boote* pairs (*Rotten*) coordinated their attacks and then quickly withdrew from the arms of British escort ships. Sailors on escort ships failed to cope with the situation and to organize an adequate defence against the extremely rapid raid of German torpedo boats. One after the other, British merchant ships soon lit up the night and sank after being hit by German torpedoes. During that night, five transport ships with a total displacement of 7,113 tons were sunk. Despite the presence of five destroyers, the ML-456 and ML-478, and the MGB-75, the British sailors were unable to respond and protect their ships, which were capable of far fewer knots than the 'devilish' *Kriegsmarine* vessels.

At the end of 1942, the *Schnellbootwaffe* on the Western Front had managed to perform a deadly strategy that succeeded in sinking 43,000 tons of Allied ships. The British, for their part, managed to strengthen their defensive potential and gathered known forces to protect trade traffic along their east coast: 45 MGBs, 24 MTBs, 35 MLs, including 20 MGBs, 7 MTBs and 17 MLs deployed in the port of Dover, where 21 destroyers and 7 corvettes were anchored, ready to react quickly to any new danger. In the southern sector of the English coast, the British had 6 SGBs (steam gun boats), 15 MGBs, 16 MTBs, 28 MLs, and 4 destroyers stationed in Portsmouth, as well as 8 MTBs, 19 MLs and 7 destroyers anchored in Plymouth.

Chapter 6

American Intervention (1943)

In early 1943 the *Kriegsmarine* was, in theory, able to assemble ninety *S-Boote* vessels. In fact, the Germans could only send seventy-four *S-Boote* to operational missions, while the other sixteen were used to train new *S-Boote* crews. On 1 January, the flotillas were in the following locations: the 1st flotilla was in the Black Sea, the 2nd, 4th, 5th and 6th flotillas took part in operations on the Western Front, the 8th flotilla was located in Norway, and the 3rd and 7th flotillas were operating in the Mediterranean.

Battleship HMS *Anson* during shooting exercises in the North Sea.

Crossing the line certificate (commemorating a sailor's first crossing of the Equator) by which the signatories became members of the crew of the battleship HMS *Anson*.

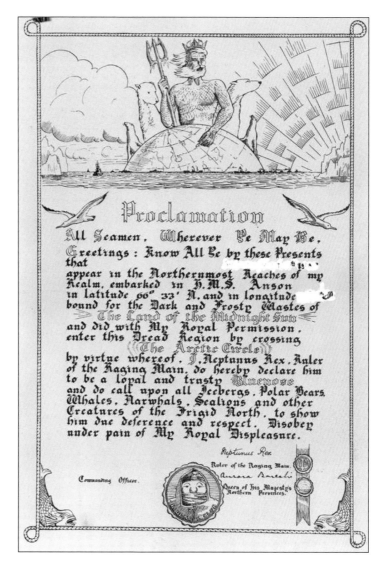

Proclamation

All Seamen, Wherever Ye May Be, Greetings : Know All Ye by these Presents that

appear in the Northernmost Reaches of my Realm, embarked in H.M.S. Anson in latitude 66° 33' N. and in longitude bound for the Dark and Frosty Wastes of *The Land of the Midnight Sun* and did with My Royal Permission, enter this Dread Region by crossing *The Arctic Circle* by virtue whereof, I, Neptunus Rex, Ruler of the Raging Main, do hereby declare him to be a loyal and trusty Bluenose and do call upon all Icebergs, Polar Bears, Whales, Narwhals, Sealions and other Creatures of the Frigid North, to show him due deference and respect. Disobey under pain of My Royal Displeasure.

Neptunus Rex
Ruler of the Raging Main.

Aurora Borealis
Queen of His Majesty's Northern Provinces.

Commanding Officer.

If we take into account those vessels that were under repair, the actual number of *S-Boote* ready for action was even less: fifty-four. As far as the British were concerned, the relationship between them and the Germans had now been reversed. The Coastal Force had 9,000 men and 1,300 officers at its disposal who were deployed on 263 operational-ready vessels of the same type (85 MGBs, 61 MTBs, 111 MLs and 6 SGBs). Given the numerous successes of the Germans during the last months of 1942 along the south-east coast of England, the British Admiralty fully understood the value of coastal forces in conflicts against the Germans and their allies. Therefore, the British made great efforts, both quantitatively and qualitatively, to strengthen their forces. The diversity between MGB and MTB vessels had almost ceased to

Above left: Admiral Sir Henry Harwood, Commander-in-Chief in the Mediterranean (31 August 1942, Alexandria).

Above right: Admiral Sir Max K. Horton, KCB DSO, Commander in Chief Western Approaches, in his office at Derby House, Liverpool, which overlooks the Operations Room (not in view).

exist. The latter of these had now been fitted with torpedo launching tubes and their auxiliary weapons which been upgraded. Both types of vessel had been given 37- or 57-mm guns at the bow and two 20 mm guns at the stern, making their crews well-prepared for the showdown with the *S-Boote* crews.

6.1. The naval battles continue

Operations resumed in early January 1943. In the early afternoon of 5 January, *Luftwaffe* aircraft spotted a large convoy in a sector near Cromer. Half an hour later, the 2nd, 4th and 6th flotillas sent sixteen *S-Boote* with the aim of intercepting the British convoy. They were later joined by five other torpedo boats from the 5th *S-Boote* flotilla, whose vessels sailed from the port of Cherbourg to contribute to the greater success of the attackers. However, bad weather meant that all of the German vessels were forced to return to their bases. Although some *S-Boote* operations were carried out later that month, they were not as successful as they had

Aerial view of the Altafjord, where the German battleship *Tirpitz* was spotted.

previously been. On the night of 8-9 January, the crew of the "S-104" (*Oberleutnant zur See* Ullrich Roeder) ran into a mine, and the damage was so great that the crew was forced to abandon the vessel. On 18 January, the same thing happened to the "S-109" during the actions of the 4th, 2nd and 6th *S-Boote* flotilla in battles north-west of Cromer, in which almost all of their vessels took part. Despite the damage, the crew of the "S-109" managed to return their vessel safely back to IJmuiden. On 24 January, the Germans launched a new attack, but British ML-type vessels, assisted by the destroyers HMS *Windsor* (D-42) and HMS *Mendip* (L60), managed to keep them at a distance and so they were unable to endanger the British convoy.

The Germans undertook new operations during mid-February. On the 18th, three flotillas with a total of fifteen vessels participated in mine-laying missions in the waters

British submarine HMS *Thunderbolt*, 7 February 1943.

around the ports of Great Yarmouth and Sheringham, but the British were waiting for them. First, the German crews experienced an airstrike by *Fairey Albacores* aircraft that dropped five bombs on torpedo boats from the 2nd *S-Boote* flotilla, but without much success. Sometime later, the "S-71" was attacked by the destroyers HMS *Garth* (L20) and HMS *Montrose* (D01), as well as the sloop *Kittiwake* (L30) and a group of MGBs vessels, which were waiting in a trap near Great Yarmouth, thinking that German vessels would carry out an attack on their sector. The "S-71" received several hits and its engine was damaged. Finally HMS *Garth* rammed into the German vessel and broke it in two. Seventeen members of the "S-71" crew were killed in that naval clash. On 20 February, the vessels of the 5th *S-Boote* flotilla stationed at the port of Le Havre (the "S-81", "S-77" and "S-65") were transferred to the port of Cherbourg. During the afternoon of 26 February, *Luftwaffe* reconnaissance aircraft spotted a convoy carrying twenty ships, escorted by protection from five destroyers in the Start Point sector. The convoy was sailing towards the port of Leer. The "S-77", "S-65", "S-85", "S-81" and "S-68" sailed quickly with the aim of intercepting the British at sea. Several merchant ships were unsuccessfully attacked, but the first strike was scored by the crew of the "S-85", commanded by *Oberleutnant zur See* Erich Kolbe. In that attack, the LCT-381 was severely damaged. The Germans even managed to come alongside an enemy vessel and capture part of the enemy crew. Meanwhile, the "S-65" managed to launch the last missile that sank a ship in British service. Another pair (*Rotten*) of German torpedo boats ("S-68" and "S-8") sank the British steamship *Moldavia* (4,858 tons), east of Berry Head, and during that attack two armed trawlers were also sunk: the Norwegian *Harstad* (258 tons) and the British *Lord Hailsham* (445 tons).

Radars

The Metox Fumb radar was designed by a team of technicians led by Admiral Sturmel, the Kriegsmarine transmissions director, after the Germans were able to recover a Leigh projector and its radar from an English plane shot down by Flak. These devices were being used after 1942 by the planes of the Coastal Command tracking "U-Boote" in the Atlantic. The system was triggered automatically as soon as a submarine was spotted on the surface at a distance of less than 2,000 meters.

Sturmel's team used this model to create the Metox, operational at the end of 1942 on the most vulnerable Kriegsmarine ships, notably the "U-Boote" and "S-Boote". During the winter of 1943 the "S-Boote" started to be fitted with the "Hohentweil", an improved version of the Metox radar. The principle was the same: a passive radar designed to determine if a boat had been detected by the enemy, but with no way of pinpointing the danger precisely. The last version, developed in 1944, was Naxos, with identical characteristics. In spite of their inventiveness, the German engineers were unable to create a ship radar capable of indicating the exact position and direction of Allied planes and ships.

In March 1943, the month named after the Greek god of war Ares (Mars in Roman mythology), chess pieces began to be deployed in favour of the British, while the Germans encountered major problems. On 4 March, the 123rd *Luftwaffe* reconnaissance group reported to Petersen's headquarters that it had noticed a group of fifteen vessels located at 15° N and 4° W. Six German torpedo boats from the 5th *S-Boote* flotilla sailed out to sea, but their crews were unable to locate the convoy. On their way back, the "S-68" and "S-65" collided with each other at high speed, meaning they had to be towed into the port of Cherbourg with as much haste as possible. On 5 March, the 2nd *S-Boote* flotilla operated in the same sector with the "S-70", "S-29", "S-80" and "S-89". Suddenly, the crew of the "S-70" came across a mine. The explosion also hit a reserve torpedo, which exploded, and the ship quickly sank. At the same time, ten torpedo boats from the 4th and 6th *S-Boote* flotilla were patrolling the sector around the ports of Lowestoft and Great Yarmouth, searching for targets. But the German vessels kept the crews of two enemy destroyers and sailboats at a safe distance, so they gave up undertaking an attack on the convoy. The 6th *S-Boote* flotilla decided to return to IJmuiden. The "S-74" and "S-75" were left as protectors in case British escort ships decided to take action. Then, suddenly, British aircraft appeared in the sky; four *Spitfires* and two *Typhoons*, which immediately carried out an attack on the German torpedo boats. The "S-75" was sunk during the first attack, and eleven crew members lost their lives.

The "S-74" had more luck: its crew managed to rescue their surviving comrades from the "S-75" and then successfully returned to their base with only one engine functioning. They had three dead and eight wounded.

Then, on 7 March, the final German stalemate began. The "S-119" and "S-114", as part of the 6th flotilla, came under attack by the destroyer HMS *Mackey* (D70) while operating near Great Yarmouth. At the same time, the British MTB-20 and MTB-21 suddenly appeared to assist the British destroyer. The German torpedo boats found themselves surrounded, and left the battlefield at high speed. Although they managed to avoid the British trap, travelling at a speed of more than 42 knots,

Above: HMS *Thunderbult* accompanied by a British destroyer.

Left: Three *Fairey Swordfish* aircraft armed with missiles from 774 Naval Air Squadron.

Cadets of the British Air Force at RNAS St Merry in Cornwall, February 1944. The Royal Naval Air Service St Merryn (HMS *Vulture*) is a former Royal Navy air base. It is located about 12 km north-east of Newquay and 19 km north-west of Bodmin.

they found themselves in a position that meant they failed to avoid a wild collision. The "S-119" was partially torn and its crew abandoned the vessel and transfered to the "S-114". In mid-March, four *S-Boote* flotillas which were fighting on the Western Front had only fifteen vessels ready for combat: the 2nd *S-Boote* flotilla had four operational boats, the 4th flotilla six, the 6th flotilla five, and the 5th flotilla none (the "S-20" was under repair). As the month of April brought new skirmishes with the Coastal Forces along the English Channel, the operational capacity of the Germans had never been so weak.

On 12 March, Petersen decided to concentrate his *S-Boote* flotillas in the English Channel. In October 1940, the B-Dienst had installed eavesdropping stations on the Channel Islands, and they had since sent reports of Allied naval movements sailing in and out of British ports on the south coast. The Germans were afraid of the major Allied operation planned for the month of April 1943, all because they were encouraged by the relatively successful landing of their troops at Dieppe in

Fairey Alabcores aircraft over Malta, Fleet Air Arm Station (Malta).

August the year before. The 5th and 6th *S-Boote* flotillas left IJmuiden and set off in the direction of Cherbourg. The 4th *S-Boote* flotilla took up position in Boulogne, while six operational torpedo boats from the 2nd *S-Boote* flotilla were relocated to the port of Ostend.

As had happened in previous years, when the weather improved, operations could start again. On 28 March, the 4th and 2nd *S-Boote* flotillas left the Hook of Holland and IJmuiden in order to intercept the FS 1074 convoy. The British destroyers HMS *Winsdor* (L94) and HMS *Blencathra* (L24) managed to hold the German crews of the *S-Boote* at a safe distance from the convoy. When the German torpedo boats turned to return home, a group of MGBs appeared out of nowhere and carried out a quick attack. German sailors on the "S-29" soon found themselves overpowered after a fierce encounter with the British sailors in a 'side by side' naval battle. The German torpedo boat failed to escape, and the deadly blow was dealt to it by the British crew from the MGB-333. Successive mechanical failures, Coastal Command air force, and bad weather caused the *Schnellbootwaffe* largely to fail in its efforts to endanger British convoys during the first ten days of April. But on 13 April, convoy PW 323 was spotted by two *Luftwaffe* aircraft that were part of the *Fernaufklärungsgruppe 123* (Long-Range Reconnaissance Group 123) as they were flying near Saint-Brieuc.

As soon as they received the first report, the 5th *S-Boote* flotilla sailed out to sea with six torpedo boats (the "S-81", "S-82", "S-90", "S-121", "S-112" and "S-65"). There were twenty-two British ships on the high seas, including two large tankers, traveling at a speed of about 12 knots, and the British convoy had the protection of two destroyers and three armed trawlers. The *S-Boote* crept into the sector around Lizard Point and waited for the right moment. The "S-121" first went into action at 01:03, torpedoing the British merchant ship *Stanlake* (1,742 tons). The crews of the *S-Boote* fired several torpedoes, but did not successfully hit any enemy ship. However,

Fairey Albacores over Malta.

around 02:10, the "S-90", "S-65" and "S-112" stormed the Norwegian destroyer *Exdale*, which was hit by three torpedoes and sunk after only a few minutes.

During the second half of April, the weather conditions became so bad that all operations had to be cancelled. Mine-laying missions at Berny Head and Start Point followed in May, and there were several convoy attacks.

On 21 May 1943, the *Schnellbootwaffe* headquarters left Wimereux and settled in Boulogne, and the commanders of the *S-Boote* flotillas were given new orders in June. The 2nd and 6th flotilla left Ostend and headed for IJmuiden, while the 4th flotilla was sent to Saint Peter Port. On 17 June, as they were leaving the port of Ostend and heading for IJmuiden, the "S-80"and "S-86" came under attack by British aircraft. Thanks to quick manoeuvering by winding left and right, these German torpedo boats managed to escape without major damage. On 20 June, the "S-122" and "S-90" were attacked by Coastal Command aircraft as they were returning to the Hook of Holland. The "S-90" received a hit and water began to seep into its interior. Nevertheless, two German torpedo boats managed to return to their base in the Netherlands.

Wedding ceremony of members of the Royal Navy in Harwich, December 1942.

Admiral Sir Bertram Ramsay (centre), July 1944. Ramsay was the Allied Naval Commander in Normandy (Allied Naval C in C in Normandy).

These RAF attacks along the Dutch coast were proof that the British were now much more free to pursue German torpedo boats all the way back to the French ports in the Channel, despite the presence of *Luftwaffe* aircraft, whose airports in Belgium and the Netherlands were an excellent base for air operations in those areas. Meanwhile, the RAF's more offensive tactics began to prove very effective for the British and for every German raid, they now responded equally aggressively and Petersen's pirates began to feel the effects. Things would get even worse for them when, in mid-June 1944, the Allied invasion of Normandy followed and strong air pressure was exerted by the actions of their air forces on the ports of Le Havre and Boulogne. At that time, the *Luftwaffe* were no longer the same adversary they had been in the earlier years of the war and their smaller aircraft force would not be able to counter British and American air operations.

The activities of the *Schnellbootwaffe* plummeted during the summer of 1943. A large number of vessels were in dry docks while experts installed new anti-aircraft weapons. As the constant threat from Coastal Command aircraft affected the success of the *S-Boote* flotilla's activities, Petersen and his torpedo boat commanders decided to strengthen the auxiliary weapons on their vessels. Now 40- and 37-mm guns were installed, along with 20-mm four-barrel cannons (*Flakvierling*) which, thanks to their high precision firing speed, had proven to be extremely effective against enemy aircraft that could, in low-flying action, easily threaten or sink *S-Boote*. The ammunition was now housed in more heavily protected spaces inside the torpedo boats and the artillery was better protected thanks to armoured plates. The two-barrel MG-34 and MG-42 machine guns further enhanced the defensive protection of the *S-Boote*. Similar to these alterations, the command bridge of torpedo boats was replaced by

Above and opposite: Allied preparations for D-Day.

Allied Guard, 12 April 1943 (Algeria). A British (right) and American marine guard the Supreme Commander at Allied Headquarters in North Africa, where an extremely important conference was being held.

an armoured structure (*Kalottenbrücke*), which provided much better protection for the crew from the often savage battles with sailors and pilots of the British armed forces.

6.2. The arrival of the Americans

In April 1943, three PTs (Patrol torpedo boats) belonging to the US Navy 2nd fleet arrived in Dartmouth, England. They were Higgins-78 type, 28-metres long and with 43 tons of displacement. The boats were initially used to land American agents of the OSS (Office of Strategic Services) on the coast of France, who were on missions to establish contact with parts of the French resistance movement. About twenty sorties were carried out by the units of the 2nd flotilla between mid-May and the end of 1943. At the same time, new fleets of US Navy flotillas began arriving in England: the 34th in May 1944, followed by the 35th and 30th in early June of that year, to take part in Operation *Neptune* (the invasion of Normandy). Command of these forces was entrusted to Frigate Captain John Bulkeley, who had earned his reputation during the fighting in the Philippines in January 1942 by attacking Japanese transport ships carrying soldiers in his PT-34 boat, near Bataan.

During the Second World War, the US Navy managed to build several types of high-speed torpedo boats. The best of these were the ELCO 80 and Higgins 78, of which 320 vessels of the former were built, and 205 vessels of the latter. Compared to the *S-Boote*, American torpedo boats were smaller and their maximum speed was lower than German vessels of the same category. Their auxiliary armaments, as was the case with all other forces in the war, would be greatly improved between 1943 and 1944.

In late July 1943, the Allies took the operational initiative. As German units moved between Boulogne and Ostend on 24 July, the "S-68" and "S-77" were attacked by

American and British convoy sailing for Russia, May 1942.

Allied soldiers boarding amphibious boats to take them to the African mainland during Operation *Torch*, an Allied invasion operation in North Africa (November 1942).

an MGB and MTB patrol north of Dunkirk. The "S-77" was hit several times by the MGB-40 and MGB-42, resulting in a torpedo explosion on a German torpedo boat, which caused it to sink. Only four German sailors managed to survive this accident, and they were later rescued by British sailors, while the German commander *Oberleutnant zur See* Joseph Ludwig was killed in the midst of the fierce battle. The "S-68", which also took part in the skirmish, managed to escape from the battlefield thanks to the high speed of its vessel, without thinking how it might help its comrades who were stranded at sea. *Oberleutnant zur See* Jürgen Moritzen, commander of the "S-68", later found himself in a military court where he was accused of cowardice in the face of the enemy, and was removed from the position of commander.

On the afternoon of 25 July 1943, 118 B-17 *Flying Fortress* aircraft from the US Air Force 8th bombing group dropped 522 tons of bombs on the port of Kiel.

The Americans sank two submarines, *U-395* and *U-474*, as well as the "S-44" and "S-66", which belonged to the 8th flotilla. In the morning hours of 29 July, a new US air strike took place, this time involving 139 B-17s, which suddenly appeared over a German port dropping 315 tons of bombs. The brand new "S-135" and "S-137", which had just arrived in the 6th flotilla, were severely damaged. On the afternoon of 11 August, the port of Brest also found itself under air-attack from British aircraft. Twenty-five B-26 *Martin Marauder* aircraft caused significant damage to the installations and moored vessels there. At the same time, seven torpedo boats from the 4th and 5th flotillas had left the port of Saint Peter Port a few hours earlier and sailed towards Brest, before coming under attack near Aber-Wrac'h. British planes immediately managed to kill the commander of the "S-121", *Oberleutnant zur See* Johan Konrad Klocke, and eleven crew members. Shortly afterwards, a second attack followed with four British fighter-bombers damaging the "S-117". This series of raids showed that the Allies had changed their tactics: instead of fighting the *S-Boote* at sea, they had now seen it was more effective to attack enemy bases, thus trying to prevent the *Schnellbootwaffe* offensive actions against the convoys. The increasing pressure reached its climax when the port of Le Havre was heavily bombed in June 1944.

6.3. British victories and a strengthened German defence

In September and October 1943, two violent battles took place between the British escort forces and the *Schnellbootwaffe* fleet. The first took place on the night of 24-25 September when a large German mine-laying operation, codenamed *Probestück,* was launched not far from Long Sands. All the flotillas operating on the Western Front were involved in the operation, and twenty-nine *S-Boote* were at sea that night, although the "S-87" from the 4th flotilla was forced to return to base following engine problems. Three hours later, the "S-38", "S-74" and "S-90" collided while travelling at a speed of 38 knots at a short distance from each other. The damage was great and their commanders decided it was best to return to the Hook of Holland. Around 01:00, the "S-88", "S-96" and "S-99" almost came face to face with four armed trawlers, which were part of a convoy escort. The crew of the "S-96" managed to launch a torpedo that broke through the hull of the *Franc Tireur* (327 tons), sinking the ship immediately. The British responded by sending boats ML-145 and ML-150, which were patrolling near the area of the German attack, with the aim of intercepting German vessels before they could retreat in their usual manner. The ML-145 was more fortunate as it managed to attack the "S-96" so fiercely that the British vessel struck a German torpedo boat, and the two ships now found themselves trapped next to each other. The impact was so fierce that it resulted in considerable damage, but thanks to its three diesel engines, the crew of the "S-96" somehow managed to free their vessel from the awkward situation. However, the crew of the ML-150 soon recovered and it was not long before they caught up with the German vessel and prevented it from escaping. Members of both crews now took part in bitter duels at a very short distance from each other using deck guns, until smoke appeared on the German vessel. The clash was the embodiment of the best scenes from old pirate movies. Despite a confusing battle, the Germans were able to sink their flaming *S-Boote*, which was abandoned at the last minute. Thirteen crew members were picked up by the British, and the German commander, *Oberleutnant zur See* Herman Sander, and his deputy, *Oberleutnant zur See* Wilhelm Ritter von Georg, were captured.

American soldiers in amphibious boats begin landing in Algeria.

After a three-week period in which mines were laid, further fighting ensued with units of the Royal Navy. On the evening of 23 October 1943, the *Schnellbootwaffe* headquarters issued an emergency order to its flotilla commanders. An extremely important convoy (FN1160), in which thirty-one ships were sailing, accompanied by destroyers and armed trawlers, was on its way to the mouth of the Humber River. Twenty-eight *S-Boote* from the 2nd, 4th, 5th, 6th and 8th flotillas were ready for action, but bad weather over the Channel prevented them from leaving the port. On 24 October, they again attempted to carry out an attack against the same target as weather conditions improved. Thirty-one *S-Boote* were ready for action, and it was the 6th flotilla that was the first to establish contact with the representative of the British convoy. Nine German torpedo boats split into groups of two (*Rotten*) and attempted to carry out an attack on the cargo ships, but to no avail. They were kept at a safe distance by the 40-mm guns of British crews on MGB torpedo boats. The "S-79" and "S-74" were hit on several occasions and could not take up an offensive position. *Kapitänleutnant* Witt, commander of the "S-74" had more luck and managed to sink the 235-ton armed trawler *William Stephen*.

Around midnight, the 4th flotilla was able to approach the convoy. The first attack group consisted of four German torpedo boats, under the command of *Korvettenkapitän* Werner Lützow, who decided to approach the British from the south. The second group, consisting of four torpedo boats, under the command of *Kapitänleutnant* Causemann, attacked from the west. The British were alerted to the presence of the *S-Boote* after being spotted by British airplanes returning from action near the Ruhr. The destroyers, which were alerted at the last minute, managed to deploy themselves for a successful defence. Thanks to radar from the British ship *Pytchley*, British sailors were able to detect the presence of German vessels and open fire at a distance of 2,000 metres from the enemy, which prevented the German sailors from launching a swift and sudden attack. HMS *Eglinton* was ordered to stay with the convoy to provide protection, while HMS *Worcester*, HMS *MacKay* and HMS *Campbell* rushed towards the *Pytchley* in order to provide support against the *S-Boote*. They were accompanied by torpedo boat MGBs, which provided additional protection to the British operation. The game of cat and mouse between the British and German sailors lasted for almost four hours, without either side being able to do anything meaningful. Around midnight, Causemann's "S-120" found itself attacked by HMS *Worcester*. The "S-88", "S-63", "S-110" and "S-117" swiftly arrived to help the German sailors which were under attack. But MGB-603 and MGB-607 also managed to arrive on the battlefield and provide protection to the British destroyers. This was followed by fierce fire around the torpedo boats of the 4th flotilla, which were forced to drive more slowly to avoid the risk of a collision. During the battle, the "S-63" received a hit in the engine room which caused a great deal of damage and seriously wounded four crew members. The torpedo boat was forced to reduce its speed to 20 knots. Commander Lützow tried to come to the assistance of his comrades in his "S-88", but heavy fire from the MGBs thwarted his plan.

The *S-Boote* were caught in a storm of steel. The power of the British 57- and 20-mm cannons, combined with machine guns, proved devastating at such a small distance. The deck and top sections of the "S-88" were riddled with holes, and the fire that broke out on the command bridge spread to other parts of the German vessel. *Korvettenkapitän* Werner Lützow was killed, as were the commander of the "S-88", *Oberleutnant* Heinz Raebiger, and three crew members. As the fire had not been extinguished, an explosion occurred on the "S-88", destroying the vessel in just a few minutes. The British pulled nineteen survivors to the deck of their ships.

The failure of the attack on the FN1 160 convoy convinced Petersen and his advisers to analyze the use of their previous tactics in the face of an increasingly aggressive enemy, who managed to develop more and more destroyers and torpedo boats to defend their convoys, preventing the Germans from approaching them at a distance

American and British sailors extend hands of friendship at Londonderry Naval Base, after US ships escorted convoys in the Atlantic for the first time.

A naval officer and four sailors, along with their dog 'Ighty', on the deck of their ship. The dog, sitting on a German flag, had been captured on a German tanker and broke his leg during the action near Dieppe. The bandage can be seen on its front left paw.

from which they could be dangerous. The Germans decided that it was necessary to strengthen the protection and auxiliary weapons on their vessels. In early October 1943, the Germans received a new type of torpedo, the TZ Zaunkönig, which replaced the older G7As models.

On 2 November 1943, nine torpedo boats from the 5th flotilla left the port of Boulogne on their way to intercept the CW 221 convoy spotted south of Dungeness by *Luftwaffe* aircraft. The *S-Boote* quickly found themselves on the battlefield, and the first *Rotten* to carry out the attack were the "S-112" and "S-141". However, they failed to successfully target their enemies. The "S-100" and "S-138" managed to get closer to the three Allied ships, thanks to some quick and deft manoeuvring, but failed to set up their vessels for a successful attack with their torpedoes. Those two torpedo boats manoeuvred again and this time, their torpedoes hit the targets. The steamships *Foam Queen* (811 tons) and *Storia* (1,967 tons) found themselves in flames. A third group made up of the "S-136", "S-142" and "S-143", managed to sneak up on the back of the convoy, where there were no escort ships at the time.

Above and below: Allied convoy en route to North Africa, 14 April 1943.

Once again, the German torpedo boats took up an offensive position and a torpedo hit the ship *Dona Isabel* (1,179 tonnes), which immediately caught fire.

Despite the presence of several destroyers and five MLs, the British did not respond well to the rapid German attack. Freedom of mobility, which was so characteristic of small formations of eight - ten vessels attacking in pairs, proved at the time to be the best form of Petersen's *Schnellbootwaffe*. Therefore, their headquarters decided to continue to use small groups to intercept enemy ships in convoys, instead of fighting in large groups made up of several flotillas.

The end of November 1943 was full of mine-laying operations at sea. In a relatively short period, the British lost the freighter *Cormount* (2,841 tons), which sank on 11 November after it struck a mine near Harwich. On 26 November, the steamer *Morar* (1,507 tons) was also destroyed. In December, the destroyers *Worcester* and *Holderness* were severely damaged when they hit a mine. Later in December,

Anti-submarine patrol on the Hmt *Stoke City*, November 1942.

Anti-submarine patrol, November 1942.

the "S-142", under the command of *Oberleutnant zur* Zee Hinrich Ahrens, sank the armed trawler *Avanturine*, which had been acting as an escort for a convoy. Other ships from the convoy came under heavy attack from German torpedo boats from the 5th flotilla, but the Germans did not achieve any major success. The year ended with no major operations because the weather conditions were bad and the small surface units did not have the right conditions to set sail. When considering the strong reinforcements assigned to the British convoys, 1943 left bitter memories for Petersen's pirates, as they managed to sink only sixteen ships (26,000 tons).

Chapter 7

Maritime Operations and Operation *Neptune* (1944)

On 1 January 1944, the general situation of the *Schnellbootwaffe*'s performance was as follows. The 1st *S-Boote* flotilla was in action near the Crimea from the port of Ivan-Baba on the Black Sea, with seven *S-Boote* ready for operation. The next four *S-Boote* were being repaired at the Constanţa shipyard in Romania, while the other three torpedo boats were eagerly awaiting arrival from Germany. The 2nd, 4th, 5th, 6th, 8th and 9th flotillas were stationed in IJmuiden, Rotterdam or Cherbourg, from where their *S-Boote* went on mine-laying operations or on missions to attack convoys along the east and south coasts of England. Those six *S-Boote* flotillas had forty-six operationally ready torpedo boats at their disposal.

"*S-Boote*" in the port of Ostend.

In the Mediterranean, the 3rd and 7th *S-Boote* flotillas took part in the fighting against the Royal Navy, and had also clashed with American vessels operating from Gibraltar since May 1943. The two *S-Boote* flotillas had sixteen torpedo boats at their disposal, but only half of that number were operational. The remaining eight vessels of that type were under repair in Genoa. In the end, the two *S-Boote* flotillas operating in the Baltic Sea had fifteen torpedo boats at their disposal, whose vessels were used to train new German sailors.

7.1. New *S-Boote* raids from French and Dutch ports

As usual, the weather conditions were extremely unfavourable during January 1944, and all *S-Boote* flotillas stationed on the western front remained in the dock or under the protection of their bases. As the weather improved somewhat in the second half of the week, the *S-Boote* were sent back into action. On 5 January the torpedo boats of the 5th flotilla, grouped into three *Rotten* groups, carried out an attack on the WP 457 convoy, after *Luftwaffe* reconnaissance aircraft (*Ju-88s*), submitted their reports after taking off in the late afternoon from Caen-Carpiquet Airport. In that action, German crews sank five merchant ships, with a total of 12,500 tons, while at the same time, the armed trawler *Wallase* (545 tons) was submerged. During these attacks, German sailors used new T-5 and T-4 *Falke* torpedoes for the first time, which were acoustic-guided missiles. On 30 January, the 5th *S-Boote* flotilla received orders to set sail again. The B-Dienst wiretapping stations had discovered a large convoy and seven *S-Boote* immediately set off during the evening hours on an uncertain mission. Suddenly, a radar detector called FuMB (*Funkmess-Beobachtungs-Gerat*) began to buzz loudly on the "S-112", which meant that enemy ships were located 6 miles from the Germans. At the same moment, the three *Rotten* took up their positions to carry out the deadly attack. The convoy CW 243 sailed south-east of Beachy Head without much of an escort, which would prove fatal to the British. At 02:00, another *Rotten*, the "S-138" and "S-142", attacked the rear of the British convoy. They caught the British by surprise because the German torpedo boats, thanks to the darkness, had managed to approach their targets unnoticed. From a distance of 800 metres, the "S-142" fired a torpedo at the trawler *Pine* (542 tons), which sank two minutes later, in two pieces. The next victim was the British freighter *Emerald* (806 tons), although it was missed by the first torpedo that was fired. However, another torpedo proved deadly and the ship was sunk. The crew of the "S-138" sent the steamer *Caleb Sprague* (1,813 tons) to the bottom, and during that action two other pairs of *S-Boote* had to manoeuvre to avoid the attack of two British destroyers and several MGBs. Their actions completely prevented the successful attack of the German torpedo boats on the convoy.

French destroyer *La Combattante*.

The Isle of Wight.

In early February 1944, the 2nd, 5th, 8th and 9th *S-Boote* flotillas took part in mine-laying missions near the mouth of the Humber River. These actions were carried out over a period of two weeks and during one of them, the "S-85" and "S-99" together sunk the 207-ton British trawler *Cap d'Antifer*. Nothing more spectacular happened during February: the month passed in carrying out mine-laying operations, followed by operations to intercept British convoys, in which the *S-Boote* were not so lucky. Despite the new T-3 and T-5 torpedoes, Petersen's sailors failed to achieve any success. In these operations, an average of five torpedo boats would fire twenty torpedoes in each attack, and of all the torpedoes fired, only one hit its target.

In March, the escort of British convoys was considerably strengthened. From now on, the British used several groups of MTBs accompanied by destroyers and cruisers. The Allies now took the initiative and possessed everything necessary to undertake the greatest naval operation of all time: the Channel and the North Sea soon became British again. At noon on 26 March, 344 B-26 *Martin-Maurder* bombers from the US Air Force 9th bomber fleet flew over the sky near IJmuiden at an altitude of 4,000 metres. In just a few seconds, 1,120,453 kg of bombs were dropped, which fell on huge bunkers where *S-Boote* from the 6th and 8th flotillas were hiding. Although these bombs were very powerful, they barely scratched the surface of the bunkers, penetrating to a depth of only 30 cm, which was not enough as there was still 3.70 cm of the inner layer left undamaged. Only the "S-93" and "S-129", which were in the dock for repairs during the air bombardment, were sunk by American bombs.

On 26 August, six German torpedo boats from the 5th and 9th flotillas left Boulogne during the evening hours, racing west. Their mission: to intercept Allied invading barges and gather as much information as possible about their possible movements, weapons, speed and tactical formations. On their way, the *S-Boote* were spotted by coastal radars in Portsmouth, which immediately alarmed sailors on the British frigate HMS *Rowley* and the French destroyer *La Combattante* patrolling south-west of the Isle of Wight. The two ships soon noticed *S-Boote* on their radars, which were approaching them at high speed from a distance of 3,000 metres. Two groups of torpedo boats approached Allied ships in zig-zag manoeuvres at a speed of 35 knots, releasing a smokescreen in an effort to approach the enemy and get close enough to inflict as much damage as possible. Sailors from the French destroyer were the first to open fire, targeting German vessels at a distance of 2,000 metres with their 102-mm double cannons. The "S-167" received a hit, but only minor damage was inflicted and its commander managed to pull his vessel to a safe zone. However, the crew of the "S-147" was not so lucky. A grenade exploded in the bow area, causing a fire to break out that soon engulfed the rest of the *S-Boote*. Some of the crew managed to escape in time, but the vessel sank a few minutes later. On 27 April, 30 miles from Barfleur, two MTBs managed to rescue ten surviving German sailors from the sunken "S-147".

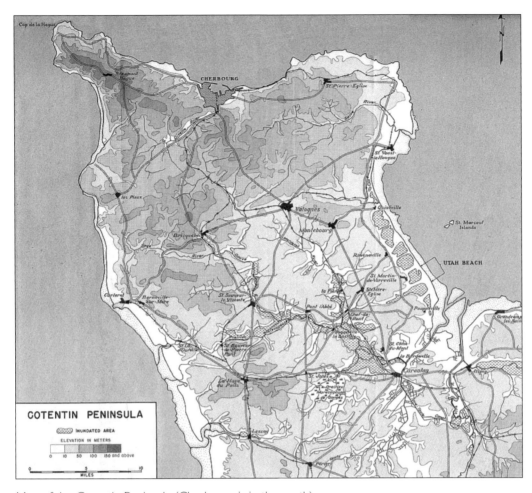

Map of the Cotentin Peninsula (Cherbourg is in the north).

DUKW in
France.

Left: Canadian "LST".

Below: US troops during Operation *Tiger*.

7.2. Allied defeat: disaster at Lyme Bay

On the afternoon of 27 April 1944, *Luftwaffe* reconnaissance aircraft alerted *Schnellbootwaffe* headquarters to a group of seven ships sailing at low speed west of the starting point at 50° north latitude and 4° west longitude. The 5th and 9th *S-Boote* flotillas were immediately put on standby, and at 22:00 the German sailors set sail from Cherbourg. At first, the Germans were unable to detect the convoy, but then almost ran into eight American LSTs (*Landing Ship, Tank*) that were travelling towards Lyme Bay at a speed of 3 knots, accompanied by only one escort ship, the frigate HMS *Azalea*. The Allied ships had just left the port of Brixham, intending to take part in landing exercises on the south coast of England. The beaches there were similar to those in Normandy on the Cotentin Peninsula, where a real Allied invasion would follow two months later. The exercise, codenamed *Tiger*, aimed to unload heavy equipment and as the LST transported tanks, jeeps and completely new types of vessels called DUKWs (colloquially known as 'ducks'), which were somewhat strange semi-amphibious and semi-tractor vehicles that were able to float on water and drive on land.

The Americans experienced a number of problems as they performed the exercises. The LSTs were very slow because their two diesel engines only had a maximum speed of 12 knots, and the vehicles they were transporting meant their load was also

British troops before the attack on the port of Le Havre (Operation *Astonia*), 13 September 1944.

Crews of British Churchill tanks observe the effect of the bombing of RAF aircraft on Le Havre.

at the maximum, giving them almost no manoeuvrability. Moreover, the LSTs were armed, which contributed even more to their weight, but their sailors relied on the destroyers to give them protection. For this exercise (*Tiger*), only one of the two British vessels was initially tasked with providing protection to transport ships. HMS *Azalea* was a corvette equipped for anti-submarine operations, and its commander and personnel never took part in the fighting against the *S-Boote*. Their inexperience

American "M-4 Sherman" tank loaded on a transport ship (LCT), just before landing in Normandy.

would thus have a major impact on the outcome of the ensuing fighting. The US Navy had only arrived in British waters a month earlier, and its sailors were deployed to their ships only two weeks previously.

At midnight, the crew from *Azalea* received a radio message from the NCC (Naval Commander in Chief) in Plymouth, who warned them of the presence of several *S-Boote* near their navigation zone. Despite the great danger, the British commander decided to proceed further and carry out the exercise as planned. At 01:30, the LST-507 detected an echo on its radar, indicating the presence of several smaller vessels approaching them from the north.

What follows is a report on the *S-Boote* attack from LST-507 officer Joham Eckstam, who was on deck at the time of the attack:

The explosion surprised us all. The effect of the torpedoes and the shock wave that followed forced me to kneel on the bridge of the ship. I was lucky, I stayed unharmed. The situation, however, was dramatic. The vessel was quiet, as if dead in the middle of the ocean. Then a fire broke out in the engine room as flames began to engulf the upper deck, where amphibians and other equipment were housed. Before leaving Brixham, all the fuel tanks were loaded, and to make the exercise as realistic as

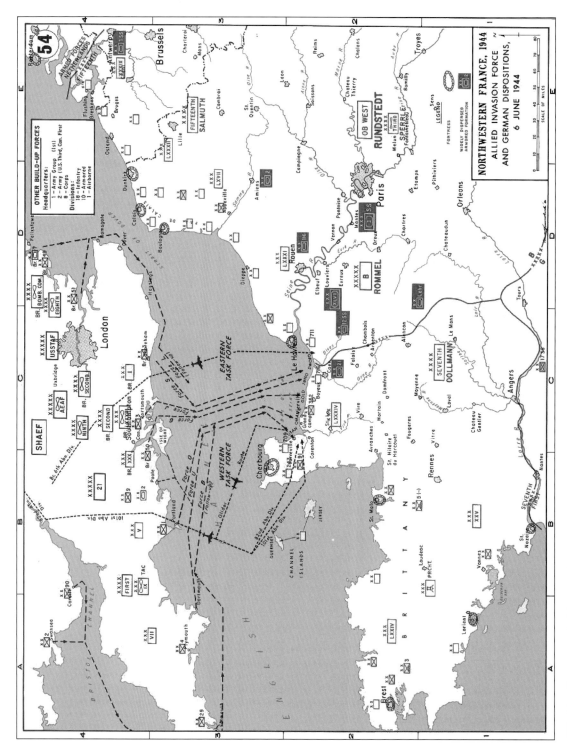

Allied landing routes in Normandy.

possible, the jeeps and Shermans were loaded with ammunition. At that moment, I had the feeling that I was looking through the gates of hell. Everything around me was engulfed in flames: the jeeps were burning, while the ammunition was causing powerful explosions, and I was listening to the shouts and moans of the people who were trapped in the deadly trap.

The burning LST-507 (1,490 tons, with a cargo of 4,000 tons) was abandoned by some of its crew. A few minutes later, two torpedoes hit the LST-531 (1,650 tons), causing the ship to sink in less than 10 minutes. At 02:28, the LST-289 (1,490 tons) was the target of a new *S-Boote* attack, but its commander reacted in a timely manner and manoeuvred to avoid destruction, then successfully returned his ship to Brixham with only one working engine. The attack claimed the lives of 197 American sailors and 441 pieces of equipment were lost. The *S-Boote* crews, it should be noted, did not help rescue the surviving American sailors (fearing a British attack), and quickly returned to Cherbourg.

Allied plans for invasion were not yet known to the Germans, but Eisenhower learned a great deal from the disaster at Lyme Bay. During a meeting the next day with General Marshall, a number of questions were asked to which an answer was urgently sought. How was it possible for such a small force to carry out an attack on American ships so easily in a zone allegedly controlled by the Allies, and only a few miles from the warships that could have intervened? How could a handful of wooden boats inflict such damage on US Navy units without the enemy suffering any damage? The British and Americans, just two months before Operation *Overlord*, had to find a quick solution if they wanted to prevent an even greater tragedy from happening in the future.

The Allied response did not help much when preparations were made in May 1944 for major air strikes on ports: Le Havre was bombed on 14 June, and Boulogne the next day. On the German side, the beginning of May was filled with mine-laying missions around the Isle of Wight and the Needles (by the 4th *S-Boote* flotilla). During the night of 12–13 May, the *Combattante* once again found itself in operations south-east of the Isle of Wight, along with the Greek corvette *Tombazis*, the British frigates *Stayner*, *Trollop* and *Stevenstone*, while further west was the corvette *Gentian*. This large concentration of vessels around Spithead and the Solent occurred due to the presence of 600 ships preparing to take part in Operation *Neptune* (naval phase of Operation *Overlord*), which was to begin three weeks later. The British Admiralty decided to use its force for two purposes: defence and mine laying. The defence against the *Schnellbootwaffe* was particularly active in April and early May 1944 in the area around the Solent. Mining was carried out primarily to protect the edges near the gulf of the Seine, where ten canals were to channel the five fleets that took part in Operation *Overlord*, directing each landing zone to the beaches of the Cotentin Peninsula.

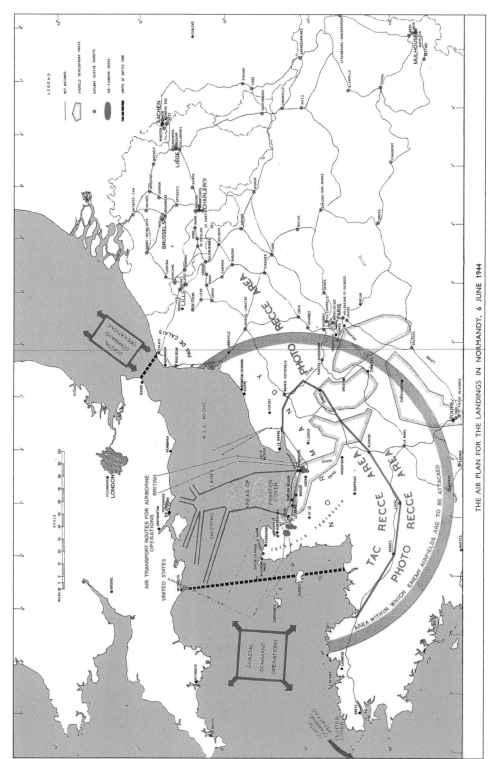

THE AIR PLAN FOR THE LANDINGS IN NORMANDY, 6 JUNE 1944

Normandy landing air support plan.

At 00:34 contact was observed on the *Combattante* at a distance of 4,000 metres; four echoes appeared on the radar screen, representing vessels approaching at high speed. The corvette, on which the flag of Free France was flying, immediately opened fire from its two 102-mm cannons, after which one *S-Boote* received a hit. On the deck of the "S-141", the crew tried hard to put out the fire that had broken out after hitting the rear of the torpedo boat. Two more grenades hit the vessel, causing the fire to ignite. A group of *S-Boote* tried to approach a French ship to fire their torpedoes, but French commander Patou performed an unexpected manoeuvre. Avoiding a German torpedo just 10 metres from his ship, Patou opened fire on the Germans while his ship was at a safe distance from the range of enemy torpedoes. After this, the *Combattante* attacked the "S-141" again, which was sunk very quickly. Seventeen crew members were killed during the fighting, including Admiral Dönitz's son, *Leutnant zur See* Klaus Dönitz, whose body was found on the French coast a few days later.

The American battleship *Arkansas* provides fire support to the troops landing on Omaha Beach.

7.3. Fighting during the summer of 1944

On 3 June 1944 (at 23:00) Petersen's headquarters in Scheveningen received information from the Marine Group West (*Marinegruppewest*) indicating that the Allied invasion would be undertaken during the night of 4 June in the area between Cherbourg and Le Havre. On the same day, 534 British and American bombers, accompanied by 447 fighters, attacked the coastal batteries along a 60 km length, starting from the French coast all the way to the Strait of Dover. They also targeted Boulogne, where there were bunkers under which the *S-Boote* were hidden, but their bombing had little effect due to the strength (and quality) of the buildings' construction.

On 5 June, from headquarters in Paris (on the corner of Boulevard Suchet and Place de Colombie), Admiral Theodore Krancke, Commander-in-Chief of the *Kriegsmarine* on the Western Front, issued an order to launch an operation codenamed *Körbchen*. All units stationed between the southern end of the Channel and Zeebruge received orders to take measures for the new level of readiness (level 2 and level 3). Despite the events that took place that day, the tensions present among the crews of the *Kriegsmarine* soon became serious. The sunny weeks of May 1944 contributed to the fact that the Germans increasingly feared an Allied invasion of Western Europe. But due to bad weather in June, when it rained heavily and the wind force was 4 Beaufort, the Germans sank into a state of relaxation, reducing their vigilance and military readiness, which was especially the case on 6, 7 and 8 June, when the forecast predicted such bad weather conditions that it was thought no major operation (let alone the largest invasion operation in history) would be possible in the area around the Strait of Dover.

Nevertheless, Petersen and his senior officers took the necessary precautions, and from the end of May the movements of their vessels were directed in a stretch from the North Sea area all the way to Cherbourg and Boulogne. New types of *S-Boote* vessels were also sent to the Channel zone, so that on 5 June 1944, the battle order of the *Schnellbootwaffe* on the Western Front looked like this:

- **The 2nd *S-Boote* flotilla was located at the Ostend base:**
  Korvettenkäpitan Opderhoff,
  "S-177", "S-178", "S-179", "S-189"
  (in repair: "S-176", "S-180", "S-182", "S-190")

- **4th *S-Boote* flotilla stationed in Boulogne:**
  Korvettenkäpitan Fimmen,
  "S-169", "S-171", "S-172", "S-173", "S-174", "S-175", "S-187", "S-188"

- **5th *S-Boote* flotilla stationed in Cherbourg:**
  Korvettenkäpitan Klug,
  "S-84", "S-100", "S-136", "S-139", "S-140", "S-142" (in repair: "S-112", "S-143")

- **8th *S-Boote* flotilla located in IJmuiden:**
  Korvettenkäpitan Zymalkowski,
  "S-83", "S-117", "S-127", "S-133"

- **9th *S-Boote* flotilla:**
  Korvettenkäpitan von Mirbach,
  "S-130", "S-144", "S-145", "S-146", "S-150", "S-167", "S-168"

Thus, Petersen had thirty-one operational vessels on the Western Front. He could count on the support of eight more torpedo boats from the 6th flotilla, whose units operated in the Baltic and were ready to leave their base if the situation on the Western Front demanded it. Opposite Petersen's *Schnellbootwaffe*, just before the invasion of Normandy, the British and Americans managed to collect twenty-eight MTBs. There were also a fleet of MGBs, twenty fleets of MLs, eleven fleets of HDMLs and four fleets of PTs. They also had at their disposal, in support, stronger naval forces that participated in Operation *Overlord* (7 battleships, 23 cruisers, 105 destroyers, 71 corvettes, 63 frigates and about 700 smaller combat units).

On 6 June 1944, at 02:34, Petersen received information at his headquarters in Scheveningen that enemy paratroopers had landed in several places on the west side of the Cotentin Peninsula. Ten minutes later, the 4th, 5th and 9th *S-Boote* flotillas received orders to provide support to the *Kriegsmarine* ships operating on the western battlefield as soon as possible. On the morning of 6 June, four German torpedo boats from the 4th *S-Boote* flotilla left Boulogne and moved to the zone between Le Tréport and Dieppe. The German sailors were already sailing far from their base when they were spotted by Allied radars, and quickly came under attack from the group of MTBs and the destroyer HMS *Obedient*. In the face of a larger enemy, the sailors on the German torpedo boats had no other option but to go back, and given the usually outstanding performance of their engines, thanks to which their vessels reached speeds of 42 knots, the Germans managed to return without a scratch.

During the night of 7 June, the 2nd *S-Boote* flotilla, under the command of *Korvettenkapitän* Opdenhoff, left Ostend with five torpedo boats ("S-177", "S-178", "S-179", "S-181" and "S-189"). They were soon joined by four more *S-Boote* from the 8th flotilla ("S-83", "S-117", "S-127", and "S-133"), which sailed from IJmuiden. Two torpedo boats were ordered to head to the Allied landing zone and attack the ships they encountered there. At the same time, the 4th *S-Boote* flotilla left Boulogne

The battleship HMS *Ramillies* bombs German positions in Normandy.

with eight torpedo boats ("S-169", "S-171", "S-172", "S-173", "S-174", "S-175", "S-187" and "S-188"). The crew of the "S-172" managed to fire a torpedo at the British destroyer, but the *Obedient* managed to avoid the attack. The 5th *S-Boote* flotilla, after its vessels arrived from Cherbourg with seven torpedo boats ("S-136", "S-138", "S-140", "S-142", "S-100", "S-139", and "S-84"), also carried out an attack on two British destroyers, but the German sailors missed the opportunity to position their vessels to carry out a successful attack. A few minutes later, the "S-139" ran into a mine that was probably dropped into the sea the day before by the sailors of MTB from the 64th fleet. Somewhat later, the 9th *S-Boote* flotilla ("S-130", "S-144", "S-145", "S-150", "S-167", and "S-168") managed to meet with some of the units from the 5th *S-Boote* flotilla in the same operating zone. During the joint operations of these elements of the two *S-Boote* flotillas, the British LST-875 (611 tons) and LCI-105 (380 tons) were sunk near Saint-Vaast-la-Hougue. The Germans lost the "S-140", which hit an English mine east of Barfleur. Attacks against Allied ships continued in the following days.

The British battleship HMS *Rodney* shells German positions near Caen.

On 8 June US sailors fell victim to an *S-Boote* attack. In the evening, the 4th *S-Boote* flotilla was operating around the mouth of the Seine. The "S-174", "S-175", "S-187" and "S-172" successfully fired several torpedoes and, despite heavy barrage fire from British escort ships, successfully sank the LST-376 (1,490 tons) and LST-314 (1,490 tons). In that same action, the destroyer USS *Meredith* (2,200 tons) was also damaged.

On 11 June, the 5th and 9th *S-Boote* flotillas set sail again. The MTB-448 was sunk in a duel with the "S-84" and "S-100", but during the "S-136"'s attack it was surprised by the appearance (east of Barfleur) of the Canadian destroyer *Sioux*, the British frigate *Duff*, and the Polish escort ship *Krakowiak*. These three Allied ships managed to send the "S-136" to the bottom. Somewhat later, north of Barfleur, the frigate HMS *Halsted* was attacked by combat pair (*Rotten*) of German torpedo boats from the 9th *S-Boote* flotilla. The bow of the frigate was badly damaged, but the ship somehow managed to reach Juno Beach.

Around midnight, torpedo boats from the 9th *S-Boote* flotilla managed to carry out an attack on several townboats pulling the artificial pontoon, Mulberry, 10 miles from Omaha Beach. After several attempts to get closer to their target, the S-Boote managed to direct their torpedos towards the USS *Partridge* (730 tons), which sank, killing thirty-two American sailors. The British townboat *Sesame* (700 tons) was also sunk a few minutes later. After this series of *Schnellbootwaffe* attacks, German sailors turned their attention to the LST convoy that was sailing towards the coast in the same sector. The LST-538 (1,490 tons) received a torpedo hit, but the ship did not sink and although significantly damaged, it managed to sail to Omaha Beach.

On 12 June, torpedo boats from the 2nd, 4th and 9th S-Boote flotillas took part in an attack on Allied ships. The "S-177" and "S-178", near the Juno Beach area, successfully sank the transport ship *Dungrange* (621 tons) during its mission of transporting ammunition. At the same time, the British steamers *Ashanti* (534 tons) and *Brackenfield* (657 tons) were also submerged during the process of delivering 660 tons of ammunition and fuel to Anglo-Canadian troops. In the evening, six torpedo boats from the 5th and 9th S-Boote flotillas left Cherbourg. Their goal was to attack the vessels in front of Utah Beach, and they planned to repeat the successful

German coastal artillery from Cherbourg 'greets' American battleships *Arkansas* and *Texas*.

operations of 7 June. The Allied defensive potential was now much stronger, and the "S-150", "S-167", "S-138" and "S-142" were confronted with several American destroyers. The "S-138" managed to get close enough to the USS *Nelson*, and the German commander, *Oberleutnant zur See* Stohwasser, successfully set up his torpedo to fire on the American ship 800 metres away. In a few seconds the torpedo was launched and it hit the bow of the American destroyer. Twenty-four sailors were killed in the blast, but the ship did not sink and was successfully towed to Portsmouth.

On 13 June, the "S-178", "S-179" and "S-189" came under air attack from *Bristol Beaufighters* from the 143rd and 236th RAF Squadrons near Boulogne, where German torpedo boats were on a mission along with the R-Boots. In that attack, three German torpedo boats were sunk, along with R-97 and R-99, without a single British plane being shot down. Despite modest successes during the first days of Operation *Neptune*, the *Schnellbootwaffe* still posed a major threat to Allied ships in their landing operations, as well as posing a lasting danger to British and American commanders, although German torpedo boats were far outnumbered by the Allied ships.

Starting on 12 June, the Operational Intelligence Center (OIC) had been sending out notices of an abnormally large group of *S-Boote* in the area around Le Havre. German sailors were apparently planning to attack Allied landing sites. Such a situation, with a fresh recollection of the May disaster at Lyme Bay, prompted the Allies to undertake several airstrikes on French coastal ports, the most devastating of which was the one against arched installations at Le Havre. This Allied mission was approved by Bomber Command, commanded by Air Marshal Arthur Harris. The air strike on the port began in the early evening hours of 14 June. A fleet of 337 aircraft, including 223 *Lancasters*, 100 *Halifaxes* and 14 *Mosquitos*, attacked the entire port facility. The first bombs exploded at 22:32, and were dropped from a height of 5,486 metres. At the same time, 22 *Lancasters* from 617 Squadron dropped their heavy bombs (Tallboys) on the docks and bunkers, where some of the vessels from the 4th, 5th and 9th *S-Boote* flotillas were located. The "S-142", "S-143", "S-144" and "S-146" were pulled ashore, and all members of their crews left their vessels, except for the crew from the "S-144", as *Oberleutnant zur See* Hans Shirren and his men were staying at a nearby station. Shirren's previous ship, the "S-145", had been badly damaged during fighting a few days earlier against American PTs. The Germans intended to carry out the action that evening and checked the engines and weapons on their vessels. At 22:30 the first shots of anti-aircraft batteries (*Flak*) followed. Shirren had only enough time to warn his men and direct them to a nearby shelter when the air bombs began to fall around the vessel. Within seconds, all hell broke loose around four *S-Boote*.

Above: The British battleship HMS *Warspite* bombs German positions in Normandy.

Left: Senior officers on deck of the *Augusta* during the Allied landings in Normandy (General Omar Bradley is on the left).

At the same time on the ship *Möwe*, the commander of the 5th *S-Boote* flotilla, *Kapitän zur See* Heinrich Hoffman, summoned his colleague Kurt Johansen, who had just taken command of the 5th *S-Boote* flotilla. They celebrated the awarding of the Knight's Cross to *Korvettenkapitän* Götz Friedrich von Mirbach. The leader of the 4th *S-Boote* flotilla, Kurt Fimmen, had just joined his comrades. At 22:32 British bombs began to fall around the German ships. In the general panic that ensued, people rushed to find rescue in bunkers or sought to climb onto their vessels to respond to the attack with gunfire. Götz von Mirbach was wounded by shrapnel in the neck and leg area, while Kurt Fimmen was miraculously spared more serious injuries. Kurt Johansen was not so lucky. He was blown away by the explosion and instantly killed. Herman Opdenhoff, commander of the 9th *S-Boote* flotilla, did not attend the party and was in a nearby villa from where he helplessly witnessed the tragedy that took place for his comrades.

At the same time, three Tallboy bombs landed on the north-west side of the bunker where the *S-Boote* were located. They pierced the top of the concrete structure, even though it was 3.5 metres thick and reinforced with metal parts. Another such bomb exploded a little further (near the middle of the bunker), causing total destruction. During the 22 minutes that the attack lasted, 1,230 tons of bombs

"S-Boote" protected by camouflage in the Dutch port of Ijmuiden, early 1944.

hit installations in the port of Le Havre. The *Kriegsmarine* lost three torpedo ships: *Falke*, *Jaguar* and *Möwe*, fourteen *S-Boote*, two *R-Boote* and twenty other vessels. Seven hundred houses were destroyed, and seventy-six civilians were killed.

On the evening of 15 June, a new air strike was carried out on Boulogne. One hundred and fifty *Lancasters*, 130 *Halifax* and twelve *Mosquitos* dropped 1,300 tons of bombs. Several R-Boote were sunk, along with fifteen other smaller ships.

During the period 7-30 June 1944, the Allies landed 850,229 men, 148,803 vehicles, and 570,505 tons of material on the beaches of Normandy. These figures represent thirteen armored divisions and thirty motorized infantry divisions.

The operational activity of Petersen's *Schnellbootwaffe* continued on the Western Front despite the heavy losses inflicted during the bombing of Le Havre. Missions continued between 16 and 19 June and included mine-laying operations or attempts to carry out attacks on convoys, which were all resolutely repulsed thanks to the strong actions of British escort ships. During the night of 22 June, seven torpedo boats from the 2nd *S-Boote* flotilla left Le Havre. The "S-190" came under attack by two British destroyers, and its commander, *Kapitänleutnant* Hugo Wendler, was forced to abandon his torpedo boat, which quickly sank following the impact of 102-mm grenades fired from British destroyers.

On the night of 23-24 June, the Germans evacuated Cherbourg, and the *Kriegsmarine* lost a very valuable operational base that the Americans would then occupy on 26 June. The movements of the *S-Boote* would continue until the end of the month. During the night of 25-26 June, the 6th *S-Boote* flotilla was transferred from Cuxhaven to IJmuiden, leaving the Baltic in favor of the North Sea, all in an attempt to strengthen the *Kriegsmarine* forces on the Western Front and to compensate for the losses suffered during the previous two weeks of fighting. A month after D-Day, *S-Boote* flotillas were still operating from three French ports, but of the twenty-three torpedo boats, only thirteen were operationally ready.

During the night 4-5 July, elements of the 8th *S-Boote* flotilla were transferred to the port of Le Havre. Around midnight, not far from La Poterie-Cap-d'Antifer, several MTBs, accompanied by the frigate HMS *Trollope*, surprised German sailors. The ensuing battle was very violent and the "S-83" received several hits that blew up its 37-mm and 20-mm cannons. Yet the Germans were able to break through to Le Havre without suffering the loss of the vessel.

On 5 July, the *Kriegsmarine* had problems again. This time there was an explosion in the torpedo depot in the port of Le Havre, which was undoubtedly a consequence of the action organized by the French resistance movement. Over forty torpedoes were destroyed, which had a direct impact on the operational capacity of the *Schnellbootwaffe* in the coming days. During the night of 8 July, all units of the 2nd *S-Boote* flotilla left Le Havre in the direction of the Seine Bay. These forces were organized into two groups: the first consisted of "S-176", "S-177" and "S-182", and the second of "S-174", "S-180" and "S-181". The first group managed to make contact with the two destroyers, which were immediately attacked. Almost simultaneously, the three torpedo boats dropped six torpedoes into the sea. At a distance of 1,400 metres the frigate HMS *Trollope* (1,300 tons) was hit in the stern. Fifty-four sailors and seven officers were killed, but the British ship, although badly damaged, was towed to the port of Portsmouth.

Bad weather reduced the fighting activity in the following days, but the fighting resumed with the same intensity from mid-July. On the night of 26-27 July, the 6th *S-Boote* flotilla left Boulogne with eight torpedo boats, under the command of *Kapitänleutnant* Metzen, rushing towards a convoy spotted by the naval intelligence service (B-Dienst) near Dungeness. Despite the presence of several MTBs and three destroyers, the "S-97" and "S-114" were in a position to launch two FA (*Flächen Absuchender Torpedo*) torpedoes from a distance of 1,800 metres. The freighters *Fort Perrot* (7,171 tons) and *Empire Beatrice* (7,046 tons) received hits, but did not sink, despite severe damage. The second *S-Boote* attack was aimed at British escort ships, but was unsuccessful. At the same time, the 2nd *S-Boote* flotilla undertook operations from the direction of Le Havre port. Near La Poterie-Cap-d'Antifer, the Germans encountered a group of twelve MTBs supported by the frigate HMS *Retalick*. German torpedo boats immediately attacked the British ships, and the crew of the "S-182" destroyed the MTB-430. The British crew, after severe damage to their vessel, had no choice but to evacuate. The operation cost the Royal Navy two MTBs, while the Germans were forced to tow the "S-182" into the port of Le Havre because of problems with its engine.

On 30 July the "S-97", "S-114" and "S-91" of the 6th flotilla left Dieppe in an effort to carry out an attack on a convoy sailing east of Eastbourne. The crews of three German torpedo boats managed to take up good positions for firing torpedoes, and launched six of them (type FA). The *Samwake* (7,219 tons) was sunk and the other four ships, the *Fort Dearborn* (7,160 tons), the *Fort Kaskaskia* (7,187 tons), the *Ocean Volga* (7,174 tons) and the *Ocean Courier* (7,178 tons), were severely damaged. Even the frigate HMS *Thornborough* was forced to intervene, firing 150 40-mm and almost 700 20-mm grenades during the battle, but none of the *S-Boote* received a hit.

An "*S-Boote*" commander before embarking on a mission.

Aerial view of Le Havre before Allied planes began the bombing in June 1944.

This once again showed the powerful speed of the German torpedo boats and reminds us how dangerous these vessels could be, despite their small numbers.

At the end of the day on 2 August, another air attack, in which fifty-four *Lancasters* from the 1st and 8th Bomber Groups took part, bombed the port of Le Havre. The "S-39" and "S-114" were sunk, while the "S-91" and "S-97" were severely damaged. On 7 August, the new 10th *S-Boote* flotilla, under the command of *Kapitänleutnant* Karl Müller, which had the "S-183", "S-184", "S-185" and "S-186" ready for operations. The "S-186", "S-191" and "S-192" left Cuxhaven in the direction of IJmuiden. On 9 August, the "S-198", "S-199" and "S-701" also arrived in the Dutch port to be assigned to the 8th *S-Boote* flotilla. Between 4 and 15 August, the 2nd and 6th *S-Boote* flotillas undertook several operations from Le Havre, during which new T3-type long-range torpedoes were used against Allied ships. On 9 August, the light cruiser HMS *Frobisher* (9,860 tons) was hit, as was the minesweeper HMS *Vestal* (960 tons), not far from Juno Beach. On 10 August, the freighter *Iddesleigh* (5,205 tons) received a torpedo hit not far from Sword Beach, as did the repair ship HMS *Albatross* (4,800 tons). In mid-August, five *S-Boote* flotillas operating on the Wesern Front had thirty-three operational torpedo boats at their disposal for Petersen's *Schnellbootwaffe*.

On 18 August, the 8th *S-Boote* flotilla spotted a large convoy in the Dover area. The steamer *Fort Gloucester* (7,127 tons) was unable to avoid the German torpedo type T-5 that hit its rear. Once again, Royal Navy escort ships were unable to drive the German torpedo boats as far away from the convoy as possible, despite the presence of five MTBs and two destroyers. On 23 August, the Germans evacuated the port of Le Havre. Within six days, over 100 *Kriegsmarine* ships, with the support of the 6th *S-Boote* flotilla, managed to pass through the blockade of British and American ships surrounding the port. The last movement took place during the night of 29-30 August, when nineteen ships left the largest port in Normandy under the protection of the 8th *S-Boote* flotilla. A German convoy was attacked by the destroyer HMS *Cattistock* and the frigate HMS *Retalick*, but the British failed to sink a single ship that day. *Korvettenkapitän* Zymalkowski and his "S-196" had managed to keep the enemy at a safe distance.

American Liberty class ship, a priority in the "*S-Boote*" attacks before D-Day.

Chapter 8

Final Battles on The Western Front (1945)

In September 1944, the 3rd and 4th *S-Boote* flotillas, the last such units stationed in the English Channel, retreated towards Rotterdam and IJmuiden.

In early September 1944, six *S-Boote* flotillas operated on the Western Front, while twenty-seven of the thirty-four such vessels were operational ready for action.

Satellite image of the port of IJmuiden.

"*S-Boote*" bunkers after the aerial bombing, February 1945.

The operations of the *Schnellbootwaffe* continued again on 5 September, mostly consisting of night mine-laying operations in the area around Cromer, while any possible attack on British and American convoys was prevented by the action of a far superior Allied air force. Petersen finally intervened personally at *Luftwaffe* headquarters in an attempt to obtain night fighters (aircraft) that would provide him with security over the sky in the areas where *S-Boote* operations would take place, but all available aircraft was prioritized to protect the actions of the Third Reich. At that time, the British Coastal Forces began operations from Dover, patrolling the coast near Dunkirk. The Germans were surrounded on land in that pocket and the only way to get their supplies was by sea using small *Kriegsmarine* ships. On several occasions, the *S-Boote* unsuccessfully tried to break the British blockade. On the night of 18-19 September, the *Kriegsmarine* performed a new operation. Two groups from the 10th *S-Boote* flotilla, under the command of *Korvettenkapitän* Müller, and transporting eight tons of ammunition, tried to break through the blockade into the port. This time the operation succeeded as four *S-Boote* managed to return to the Hook of Holland and Vlissingen, carrying the commander of the 226th Infantry Division, Lieutenant General Wolfgang von Kluge, and several of his senior officers on deck.

8.1. Withdrawal to the Netherlands and Norway

Encouraged by the success of the operation, three more *S-Boote* left the Hook of Holland to test the readiness of the British defence forces. Somewhere in the middle of their mission, German vessels were discovered by a Coastal Command reconnaissance aircraft and there soon followed an attack by the frigate HMS *Stayner* and MTB-724 and MTB-728 from the 64th fleet. The battle turned out to be extremely fierce and left no hope for the crews of the German torpedo boats. The "S-183" found itself under fire from the frigate's main guns and was immediately sunk. The "S-200" and "S-702" collided after coming under direct fire from a 40-mm projectile. Sixty surviving German sailors were picked up by the British, saving their lives.

In early October 1944, new mine-laying missions were planned, and Petersen now had twenty-one *S-Boote* vessels at his disposal, stationed at IJmuiden, the Hook of Holland and Rotterdam. On 10 October, fourteen *S-Boote* took part in a major mine-laying action at the mouth of the Scheldt in an attempt to prevent the Allies from successfully using the port of Antwerp. The Germans were soon rewarded for their bravery, as mines lying off the coast of Belgium in early November caused immense trouble to the Allies.

On 1 November, twelve *S-Boote* left the Hook of Holland during the night, rushing towards the zone near Dunkirk. Twenty-one UMBs (*U-Boot-Abwehrmine B*) and fourteen LMBs (*Luftmine B*) mines were dropped into the area, which was now

"S-216." After the war it was used by the US Navy, which left it to Denmark in July 1947 (until 1958).

"S-204" with a flag of surrender, Felixtowe (13 May 1945).

one of the most important Allied shipping routes needed to supply their troops on European soil. Four days later, the LCT-457 (600 tons) hit a mine and sank near Ostend. Then, on 7 November, LCT-976 (200 tons) became the second victim. The vessel broke in half and had to be abandoned not far from the Escaut River. On the same day, the LST-420 (2,750 tons), exploded after hitting a mine and, almost immediately, sank near Ostend.

On 1 December, the British invasion of the island of Walcheren, located near the Scheldt, provoked a simultaneous reaction from the German armed forces. Twelve German torpedo boats from three *S-Boote* flotillas stationed in the Netherlands attempted to attack British forces. But the escort ships of the Royal Navy, with the assistance of the 29th MTB fleet, successfully repulsed all German attacks. Nevertheless, the tanker *Rio Bravo* (1,140 tons) and one armed trawler, *Colsay* (384 tons), were sunk in these battles. Once the Allies took over Walcheren, the balance of power shifted in their favour. Now the sea route between the River Thames and Antwerp was under their control. On 4 December, the Royal Navy cleared the sea in front of this prominent Belgian port, which quickly became operationally ready, giving the Allies logistical support to launch a major attack on the Third Reich in the months that followed.

A captured "*S-Boot*".

Two captured "*S-Boote*".

During December 1944, mine-laying missions were carried out, but they did not go smoothly. On 15 December, six vessels from the 9th *S-Boote* flotilla left the Hook of Holland and headed for the mouth of the Escaut River. When they arrived at their desitination, they found themselves under fierce attack by the British frigates HMS *Retalick* and HMS *Thornborough*, which were accompanied by several MTBs. Although the battle only lasted a very short time, German torpedo boats were forced to leave their target zone after the "S-168" was hit several times by MTBs. With the arrival of winter, weather conditions in the North Sea became increasingly unfavourable as a wind of 8 Beaufort meant that all operations were cancelled by the second half of December 1944.

With the return of better weather the operations could continue, but now the Allies had the initiative and, more importantly, almost absolute control of the skies under which the operations were conducted. On the afternoon of 15 December, fifteen *Lancaster* aircraft of 617 Squadron undertook an almost identical raid to the one that had taken place in mid-June over the port of Le Havre. This time the target was the port of IJmuiden. A total of 69.8 tons of bombs were dropped during the 7-minute air attack, and two bombs (5.4 Tallboy) penetrated the bunker where the *S-Boote* were hiding. The "S-198" was destroyed, while the "S-193", "S-195" and "S-701" were damaged, as were four other ships. In less than 10 minutes, the entire

Unidentified German torpedo boat (class "S-26/38").

8th *S-Boote* flotilla was destroyed. Following the attack, Petersen's headquarters issued the following report:

This attack left the entire 'S-Bootwaffe' seriously endangered. It is certain that the bunkers no longer provide sufficient protection against the enemy. In the coming period, our vessels will be relocated and dispersed to our ports where they will be under camouflage protection to avoid destruction by Allied bombs.

On 29 December, sixteen British *Lancaster* aircraft bombed the port of Amsterdam again. But all German torpedo boats had already left the bunkers and were carefully camouflaged in time, saving them from destruction. The Germans had no losses this time.

The end of the year brought another defeat to the Germans. The torpedo boats "S-185" and "S-192", from the 9th flotilla, were submerged in a collision with the

"S-16". After the war, this torpedo boat was handed over to the Soviet Union.

frigates HMS *Torrington* and *Curzon*, which were assisted by the sloop *Kittiwake*, while they were on a larger mine-laying mission at Ostend. Several groups (*Rotten*) of the *S-Boote* tried to pick up the surviving German sailors, but were prevented from doing so by British escort ships. Twenty-two German sailors were rescued, but no sailor from the "S-192" was found alive. On 29 December, the 4th *S-Boote* flotilla ("S-202", "S-204", "S-205", "S-219" and "S-201") left Norwegian waters to transfer its vessels to Rotterdam.

Together with the torpedo boats from the 5th *S-Boote* flotilla, which were transferred as reinforcements, these two *S-Boote* flotillas were able to ready thirty-two vessels for action. Petersen's staff estimated that in early 1945, fifty operationally ready vessels would require 950 mines (450 LMBs and 400 UMBs), 1,600 cubic metres of fuel (1,600,000 litres) and 140 T1-G7A torpedoes.

By 9 January 1945, all operations had been cancelled due to bad weather. When it was not raining hard and very foggy, a strong wind of 4-5 Beaufort was blowing. A major mine-laying operation was undertaken during the night of 14-15 January, in the area between Dunkirk and the Humber River, and the action involved vessels from the 2nd and 5th *S-Boote* flotillas with a total of fourteen torpedo boats. During the night hours, thirty-nine mines were dropped into the sea, and on 19 January, the

It is possible that this is a torpedo boat in the class range "S-6" to "S-25."

A German torpedo boat leaves Kirkenes (Norway).

FN 6 convoy fell victim to German mines. During the defensive actions, the crew of the "S-180" ran into a UMB mine and the German torpedo boat soon sank south of the Hook of Holland.

In the night of 15-16 January, the 2nd and 5th *S-Boote* flotillas left their Den Helder base again on a mission to intercept a convoy spotted north of Cromer. The Germans undertook several attacks without suffering any losses, but failed to locate their targets accurately. Consequently, in the morning they turned back in the direction of their base. During the same night, torpedo boats from the 8th *S-Boote* flotilla ("S-194", "S-196", "S-197", "S-199" and "S-701") were sent into action. Despite suffering several air strikes by British aircraft, this time the German torpedo boats discovered Allied ships and severely damaged a British transport ship (1,625-ton LST-415). Combat operations and minefields continued, despite severe weather conditions.

On the night of 22-23 January, three convoys were again spotted in the area around the Scheldt. The 8th, 9th, 4th and 6th *S-Boote* flotillas, with a total of sixteen vessels, left the Hook of Holland and IJmuiden to inflict as much damage as possible on

HMS *Stayner*.

British and American ships. On the Allied side, the Royal Navy had forty-four MGBs, the frigate HMS *Torrington*, and the sloop *Guillemot* to provide protection for the convoy. The 8th and 6th *S-Boote* flotillas were the first to come into contact with the convoy, but the German sailors were unable to get close enough to carry out a successful attack. At 22:54, the crews of the torpedo boats from the 9th *S-Boote* flotilla still managed to break through the fire of the escort ships of the Royal Navy. At a distance of 1,500 metres, the "S-168" and "S-175" launched their four torpedoes toward a large freighter. The British steamship *Halo* (2,365 tons) was hit by two torpedoes, and after only 10 minutes it sank, dragging its crew down with it. The British reacted quickly and the frigate HMS *Stayner* and four MTBs simultaneously opened fire on two German torpedo boats, which did not have time to retreat. The "S-168" received a 76-mm grenade hit in its torpedo launcher, but although it was damaged, the German crews quickly managed to escape from the enemy thanks to the powerful diesel engines of their torpedo boats.

Left: HMS *Retalick*.

Below: HMS *Thornborough*.

During the night, the *S-Boote* flotillas tried to break through to the convoy, but their crews failed to do so thanks to good manoeuvring and precise fire from the British escort ships. At around 03:00, several vessels from the 8th *S-Boote* flotilla reached the mouth of the Thames near Tongue Sands Fort and the coastal artillery based there. Suddenly, the Metox Fumb on the "S-701" started buzzing, which meant that there were ships at a distance of 6,000 metres. Five *S-Boote* immediately headed at full speed in that direction, whose crews hoped to intercept the Allied convoy. The silhouettes of British ships suddenly became visible at a distance of less than 1,500 metres, and within just a few seconds, ten torpedoes were launched simultaneously from German vessels. All of the torpedoes missed their targets, but two destroyers and several groups of MTBs set out to deal with the Germans. As was usually the case in such direct battles, everything happened extremely quickly, with heavy gunfire from both sides. The German crews of the "S-701" and "S-199" collided with each other, and the "S-199" was so badly damaged that it had to be abandoned, while the "S-701", thanks to its powerful engines, managed to avoid destruction. The coastal artillery at Tongue Sands Fort managed to sink the abandoned "S-199" a few hours later. The British MTB-495 was also badly damaged during these battles.

Due to the daily activities of the *S-Boote* and the losses suffered (primarily caused by German mines), the British unit in charge of planning bomber operations (Bomber Command) decided to launch fresh action on IJmuiden. On 3 February, between 04:07 and 04:11, seventeen *Lancaster* bombers from the 9 Squadron dropped seventeen 5.4-ton bombs (Tallboys) onto the bunkers below, which usually housed the *S-Boote*. The second air attack followed on 8 February, involving fifteen *Lancaster*s from 617 Squadron. In that attack, the same type of bombs were used against the same target. The Germans, however, had learned their lesson from Le Havre, and had deployed their vessels at a safe distance with excellent camouflage protection. This meant that the Germans suffered no losses during these two airstrikes. Despite their numerical inferiority, the sailors on the *S-Boote* still posed a serious threat to the Royal Navy. Although the number of newly built Royal Navy escort ships had increased, and although the Allies controlled the skies, the presence of these small and fast torpedo boats in the paths of the convoys, where they continued to undertake daily offensive action, would create a real problem for the Allied High Command right up to the end of the war.

Minesweeping missions continued during February 1945. On the night of 18 February, the 2nd *S-Boote* flotilla operated in the sector around the Humber, where twenty mines were laid. Five days later, the *Combattante* patrolled north of Norfolk along with two MTBs. Around 11:45, at a buoy site near East Dudgeon, a French ship was halved in a wild explosion. The magnetic mine, which was located

Tallboy, 5,500 kg heavy bomb.

20 metres below the surface at the moment the ship was sailing directly above it, caused the death of 64 sailors, while 120 crew members were rescued by the timely arrival of British ships. Among those rescued was Pépin Lehalleur, the commander of a French ship that had sunk the "S-147" and "S-141" less than a year earlier.

On 25 February, the armed trawler *Aquarius* (187 tons) became the next victim. Three days later, the freighters *City of Lincoln* (8,039 tons) and *Cydonia* (3,517 tons) were also severely damaged when they encountered German mines. Six flotillas with a total of twenty-two torpedo boats left their Dutch bases during the night of 22 February. They set out for the east coast of England on a mission to intercept the FS 1734 convoy, whose ships were sailing north-east of Great Yarmouth. The 2nd and 5th *S-Boote* flotillas were the first to attack, with nine torpedo boats racing in the dark at a speed in excess of 38 knots. The British freighters *Goodwood* (2,780 tons) and *Blacktoft* (1,109 tons) were sunk by the action of German vessels, while the Norwegian steamship *Skjold* (1,345 tons) was severely damaged. Meanwhile, the 8th *S-Boote* flotilla attacked a small convoy of landing ships at the mouth of the Thames and sank the LCP-707. However, the Germans lost the "S-193", which was destroyed by British escort ships. The torpedo boats of the 4th, 6th and 9th *S-Boote* flotillas managed to lay mines in the sea between the Thames and the Escaut. Despite the fact that British aircraft flew over German torpedo boats several times, the crews

Concrete submarine bunker in Hamburg after a Tallboy bomb dropped from Allied aircraft, April 1945.

of the *S-Boote* successfully completed their mission and returned to their bases in the Netherlands. Mine-laying operations would continue without major disruption until the end of February 1945.

During the night of 28 February, four torpedo boats from the 4th *S-Boote* flotilla headed for the mouth of the Scheldt River. In less than 20 minutes, twenty UMB mines disappeared into the icy waters of the North Sea. At 23:00, when their mission was over, the Germans travelled to Rotterdam, sailing at a speed of 25 knots. But the British were waiting for them. The destroyer HMS *Cotswold* and the frigate HMS *Seymour* opened fire from their main guns. The "S-220" was hit in the engine room, which caused a fire to engulf the rest of the vessel. The German commander, *Kapitänleutnant* Dross, immediately issued orders to abandon the ship, which soon sank, but the crew was rescued by a British escort ship. The outcome of the battles in February were as follows: two freighters were torpedoed by the *S-Boote* for a total of 3,889 tons, while ten other Allied ships (19,551 tons) were lost as a result of their collisions with mines near the Belgian and Dutch coasts. All of this happened just two months before the capitulation of the Third Reich, which shows that the *Schnellbootwaffe* on the Western Front was still a great threat to the Allies. According to the Home Fleet report of 1 May 1945:

Attacks of German torpedo boats against our convoys have increased during the last three months, notably by the use of new and more daring approach techniques. Our enemies use two or three boats operating in small independent groups, which makes the possibility of interception by our escort ships increasingly difficult. The action of the Coastal Command planes, in spite of regular sorties and a total absence of enemy aircraft, is unable to stem the offensives off Kriegsmarine units. In spite of a power ratio unfavourable to them, they represent a constant threat to our maritime traffic.

During March, 131 defensive actions followed, and several convoys came under attack by German torpedo boats. On the night of 18-19 March, the "S-705" and "S-706" were patrolling off Lowestoft, together with other vessels of the 6th *S-Boote* flotilla. After the mine-laying mission, the German torpedo boats attacked the convoy FS 1759, and the Allies lost two freighters (3,968 tons) in the fighting. The next day, the *S-Boote* from the four flotillas repeated the mission from the previous day, in the area of the rivers Thames and Escaut. Sea mines caused the sinking of British transport ships *Samselbu* (7,523 tons) and *Empire Blessing* (7,062 tons) on 19 March. The next day, the British transporter LST-80 (2,750 tons) and the American Liberty Ship, *Hadley F. Brown* (7,176 tons), were sunk. Such a successful series continued until 22 March, when three more ships were sunk: the Greek *Eleftheria* (7,247 tons), the Liberty Ship *Charles D. McIver* (7,176 tons) and the British ML-466 (75 tons).

Avro Lancaster.

On 26 March, torpedo boats from the 4th *S-Boote* flotilla operated in the Thames-Scheldt area. Despite repeated attempts by destroyers and the group of the MTBs to intercept them, two hours after leaving their base, four German torpedo boats managed to lay sixteen UMB mines, which would cause the sinking of three Allied ships two days later. The British reacted during the night of 27 March, when three *Bristol Beaufighter* aircraft from 236 Squadron launched a rocket attack against elements of the 2nd *S-Boote* flotilla north of Texel Island. The "S-181" received several hits on the command bridge and section VII, where the fuel tanks were located. *Kapitänleutnant* Hermann Opdenhoff, the leader of the 2nd flotilla, who was on the boat to take part in the action, was killed instantly, as was the commander of the "S-181", *Oberleutnant zur See* Martin Schlenck, and four crew members.

On 6 April, despite losses in the previous two weeks, the 2nd *S-Boote* flotilla went into action again with a new commander, *Kapitänleutnant zur See* Hugo Wandler. The six torpedo boats attempted to intercept a convoy spotted at the mouth of the Humber River. Two British escort ships, the frigate HMS *Cubitt* and the destroyer HMS *Haydon*,

HMS *Torrington*.

successfully prevented German vessels from approaching the convoy. Faced with an opponent who would be numerically stronger, the crews of the *S-Boote* decided to withdraw, but before that they dropped thirty-six LMB mines into the sea. The torpedo boats were sighted by a Coastal Command Wellington aircraft, which immediately radioed the news to three MTBs belonging to the 22nd fleet, whose vessels operated from the base at Lowestoft. It took British vessels only 20 minutes to suddenly appear in the centre of the German formation. The fighting lasted an hour and a half. The MTB-494 and MTB-493 fought so close to the "S-176" and "S-177" that in the end they collided, causing huge casualties on both sides. The "S-176" immediately sank, along with the MTB-494, after both vessels caught fire. The situation with the "S-177" was no better. The commander of that torpedo boat, *Oberleutnant zur See* Karl Boseniuk, was seriously wounded by gunfire from the MTB-497, and his crew was forced to abandon ship. The British managed to tow the MTB-493 back to Lowestoft, but the vessel remained unusable.

HMS *Curzon*.

The next night, despite the losses suffered from the previous day, the Germans took action again. Fourteen boats from the 4th and 6th *S-Boote* flotillas successfully laid fifty-two mines on the line used daily by the Allies in the Thames-Scheldt area. During the mission, the MTBs again tried to intercept enemy vessels. The "S-202" and "S-703", which were sailing at maximum speed in order to avoid contact with the enemy, failed to avoid a collision.

The last defensive action in the area of the IJmuiden basin was carried out by the *S-Boote* during the night of 12 April. Twelve torpedo boats, including some vessels from the 4th, 6th and 9th *S-Boote* flotillas, carried out a mission of laying forty-eight mines near the northern part of the Flessingen chanel. The Royal Navy immediately raised the alarm and several MTBs, accompanied by the destroyer HMS *Hambledon* and the frigate HMS *Ekins*, set out to respond to the German danger. The "S-205" was hit by a 76-mm grenade that exploded in Section VI, damaging the radio cabin. Meanwhile, despite considerable damage, the commander of the "S-205", *Kapitänleutnant zur See* Hans Jürgen Seeger, managed to pull his vessel out of the combat zone thanks once again to the extraordinary and powerful MB 511 engines, which allowed him a speed greater than 41 knots.

HMS *Cotswold*.

The situation deteriorated dramatically for the Third Reich from early April onwards. On 3 April, Münster was liberated, then, on 10 April, Essen and Hanover. By the middle of the month, the Ruhr had been invaded and 320,000 men of Army Group B had capitulated. Meanwhile, the Netherlands was about to be liberated by the British and American armies. However, the situation for the *Schnellbootwaffe*, when compared to the rest of the German war machine, was not so bad. Twenty-one torpedo boats at Dutch bases were operationally ready, but they lacked fuel, torpedoes, and spare parts. Nine torpedo boats were anchored in the Norwegian port of Egersund until the capitulation of the Third Reich in May 1945. They belonged to the 8th flotilla ("S-195", "S-302", "S-303" and "S-709"), while the other five torpedo boats ("S-62", "S-79", "S-86", "S-89" and "S-133") were used for training (1st *S-Boote* flotilla). Between January and the end of April 1945, the German torpedo boats destroyed thirty-one transport ships, which were sunk mostly thanks to the mines laid along the Allied convoy shipping lanes, for a total of 88,971 tons.

S.W. Roskill, a British naval historian, points out the following:

The S-Boote were remarkably designed and their crews fought valiantly up until the end of the war. If they had been used with efficient support vessels and in tight collaboration with the Luftwaffe planes, they could have caused much greater losses to our shipping. The tenacity and the crusading spirit of their crews made them respectable adversaries.

On 13 May, two torpedo boats from the 4th *S-Boote* flotilla, the "S-204" and "S-205", made their last voyage crossing the North Sea on their way to England. They left their base at Den Helder at 9:00, and with them was Admiral Erich Alfred Breuning, who was to sign the surrender of the German naval forces stationed in the Netherlands. He was accompanied by *Korvettenkapitän* Kurt Fimmen, leader of the 4th flotilla, and *Kapitänleutnant* Bernd Rebensburg, Petersen's chief collaborator in planning naval operations. The British sailed from Felixstowe at the same time, accompanied by ten MTBs, to meet the Germans at the South Fall buoy and escort them to their destination. At the meeting point, several British officers crossed over to the "S-205". One of them, Captain Peter Scott, left the following testimony of the journey:

We still had a few dozen miles to cover before arriving in Felixstowe. This was the first time I had sailed on an enemy boat and I was immediately impressed by the size of the S-Boote. The general silhouette was hardly visible above the surface of water,

HMS *Hambledon*.

and everything seemed to have been designed to offer minimum resistance to the elements and maximum protection for the crew when the boat was travelling at full speed. In spite of the rolling, we soon reached 30 knots. The MTBs behind us couldn't keep up, and in spite of the speed we kept perfectly dry, while my comrades on our boats had to pull on their oilskins.

The *Kriegsmarine* launched 239 *S-Boote* into service between 1939 and 1945. Of all these vessels, ninety-nine survived the war intact. One hundred and twenty-seven vessels were sunk or unrepaired throughout the areas where the *Schnellbootwaffe* operated. Of the ninety-nine remaining vessels, thirty-four surrendered to the United Kingdom, thirty to the United States Navy, which in 1947 ceded fourteen to the Norwegian Navy and thirteen to the Danish Navy. The Soviets demanded twenty-eight of these vessels as war reparations. In 1951, the British Navy returned the "S-130" and "S-208" to the new German Navy (*Bundesmarine*), which ended their service as training ships.

In the period from 1939 to 1945, 7,500 officers and sailors participated in the *Schnellbootwaffe*. Among them were 149 officers, 860 non-commissioned officers and 4,639 sailors who participated in operations on the Western Front. The losses amounted to 767 dead or missing, 620 wounded, while 322 men ended the war in Allied POW camps.

On 13 May 1945, when Admiral Breuning, accompanied by his senior officers, stepped off the "S-204" onto Felixstowe pier, a ceremonial unit of the Royal Navy greeted them with an honorary salute.

HMS *Ekins*.

Glossary

B-Dienst: *Funkbeobachtungsdienst:* German Navy radio-listening services.

CMB: Coastal Motor Boat.

Coastal Forces: British command structure including MTB, MGB, ML and HDML units during WWII.

DSC: Distinguished Services Cross.

DSM: Distinguished Services Medal.

DSO: Distinguished Services Order.

E-Boat: Enemy Boat: the British term for the "S-Boote".

EMA: *Einheitmine type A:* Standard type A mine.

EMB: *Einheitmine type B:* Standard type B mine.

EMC: *Einheitmine type C:* Standard type C mine.

Enigma machine: an encryption device developed and used in the early- to mid-20th century to protect commercial, diplomatic and military communication. It was employed extensively by Nazi Germany during the Second World War, in all branches of the German military.

Fährprahm: Flat-bottomed craft invented by the Germans and used mostly during operations in the Mediterranean for supply and personnel transportation.

FAT: *Flächen Absuchende Torpedo:* circular-search torpedo.

FdT: *Führer der Torpedoboote:* Torpedo-boat leader.

FdS: *Führer der Schnellboote:* Gunboat leader.

Flak: *Flugabwehrkanone:* Anti-aircraft gun.

FMA: *Flubmine type A:* Type A floating mine.

FMB: *Flubmine type B:* Type B floating mine.

FUMB: *FunkeBeobachtunggerät:* Microwave radar equipping the "S-Boote".

G5: Soviet torpedo-launching gunboat.

HDML: Harbour Defense Motor Launch.

Kalottenbrucke: Armored pilot's bridge: to protect the crews during battle, the "S-Boote" bridge was armoured from the beginning of 1943 onwards.

Kriegsmarine: On 21 May 1935, the German fleet changed its name and became the Kriegsmarine. The old flag with the colors of the German Empire and the Maltese cross was replaced by a new flag with a swastika in November 1935.

Lauertaktik: "S-Boote" attack tactic with the boats separated into two half-flotillas, each one composed of several "S-Boote" pairs (*Rotten*).

LCA: Landing Craft Assault.

LCI: Landing Craft Infantry.

LCT: Landing Craft Tank.

LMA: *Luftmine type A:* type A aerial mine.

LMB: *Luftmine type B:* type B aerial mine.

LUT: *Lage Umgehung Torpedo:* Zigzag-search torpedo.

LSI: Landing Ship Infantry.

LST: Landing Ship Tank.

MAS: *Motoscafi antisommergibili:* Anti-submarine motor boat used in the Italian Navy.

Metox: Electronic radar detection device invented by the Germans.

MGB: Motor Gun Boat.

ML: Motor Launch (coastal patrol boat).

MTB: Motor Torpedo Boat.

MS: *Motosiluranti:* Torpedo gunboats similar to the MAS used by the Italian Navy.

Nautical mile: distance equivalent to 1,852 m.

Oberkommando der Marine (OKM): Commander in chief of the German Naval Forces.

Operation *Barbarossa*: Code name for the German invasion of the USSR.

Operatipon *Dynamo*: Code name for the Allied evacuation of Dunkirk.

Operation *Husky*: Allied invasion of Sicily.

Operation *Neptune*: Allied code name for the naval phase of "Overlord".

Operation *Overlord*: Allied code name for the invasion of Europe in June 1944.

Operation *Seelöewe*: German project for the invasion of England.

Operation *Torch*: American invasion of North Africa.

Operation *Weserübung*: Code name for the German invasion of Norway.

Percuteur: On a torpedo the metal hammer that sets off the detonator.

PT: US Navy Patrol Torpedo Boat.

Reichsmarine: Created on 31 May 1931 by the Weimar Republic to replace the provisional navy. Its role was to protect German territorial waters with a small number of vessels.

RNR: Royal Navy Reserve.

RNVR: Royal Navy Volunteer Reserve.

R-Boote: *Raumboote:* mine-sweeper.

S-Boote: *Schnellboote:* armed motorboat.

S-Boot-Bunker: Concrete structures built by Germans to protect the "S-Boote" flotillas.

S-Bootwaffe: The command structure of all "S-Boote" units.

Stichttaktik: Attack tactic which replaced the Lauertaktik. The "S-Boote" pairs operated in a single group and launched their torpedoes simultaneously.

Tallboy: Huge British bombs invented by engineer Barnes Wallis and his team, and used from May 1944 in the Royal Air Force's 617 Squadron of Lancasters.

TMA: *Torpedomine type A:* Type A anti-ship mine.

TMB: *Torpedomine type B:* Type B anti-ship mine.

U-Boote: *Untersee-Boote:* submarines.

UMA: *U. Boot-Abwehrmine type A:* Type A anti-submarine mine.

UMB: *U. Boot-Abwehrmine type B:* Type B anti-submarine mine.

Selected Bibliography

HÜMMELCHEN, Gerhard, *Die deutschen Schnellboote in zweiten Weltkrieg*, Verlag Mitller und Sohn, 1996.

FOCK, Harald, *Die deutschen Schnellboote 1914-1945*, Koehlers Verlagsgesellschaft Hamburg, 2001.

JACKSON, Robert, *Kriegsmarine: The Illustrated History of the German Navy in WWII*, Avro Press, 2001.

DALLIES-LABOURDETTE, Jean-Philipe, *S-BOOTE: German E-boats in Action 1939-1945*, Historie & Collections, 2006.

IRELAND, Bernard, *Naval History of World War II*, HarperCollinss, London, 1998.

MAX, Schultz Herbert, *Die deutsche Schnellbootwaffe im zweite Weltkrieg*, Erlangen, 1987.

SHOWELL, Jack P. Mallmann, *German Navy Handbook 1939-45*, Sutton Publishing, 1999.

WILLIAMSON, Gordon, *German E-boats 1939-45*, Osprey, Oxford, 2002.

WILLIAMSON, Gordon, *E-Boat vs MTB – The English Channel 1941-45*, Osprey, Oxford, 2011.

About the Author

Hrvoje Spajić was born in 1973 in Zagreb, where he gaduated with a degree in History from the Faculty of Philosophy. He is the author of over 150 popular-science articles and the author of eight books in the field of military history. Hrvoje is one of the scientific associates in writing the General Encyclopedia of *Leksikografski Zavod Miroslav Krleža*. According to the current field of research, his work is characterized primarily by polemology.

His other works (in Croatian) include *Waffen-SS: The Dark Forces of Criminal Politics-Soldiers of National Socialism 1933-1945*; *Great Islamic Conquests 632-750*; *Byzantium and War: Basic Military and Warfare Features of Byzantine Society 600-1453*; *Roman Army: Lord of the Battlefields of Antiquity-The Essence of Roman Militarism*; *The Beginning of the Clash between East and West: The Genesis of Military Theoretical Systems in the Ancient World*; *Waffen-SS: Hitler's Stormtroopers of Death-Operations and Organization 1939-1945* and *Crusades: Templar's perspective – Strategies and Major Battles during the Epochal Conflict between Islam and Christianity* (2020).

In addition to writing, he also illustrates books and has translated (into Croatian) Randall Wallace's novel *Braveheart*. His artistic passion is making historical maps, studying symbols and ancient scriptures. His other areas of professional interest include cryptography, cosmology, astrology, paleocontacts, mythology, occultism, Hermeticism, mysticism, holism, alchemy, Gnosticism, Kabbalah, Freemasonry, corporatism, imperialism, globalism and dictatorships. In 2019 he started his own blog about history at Parlatoria.com (World of Stories).

In his spare time he plays guitar and sings (he has been a member of the Academic Choir *Ivan Goran Kovačić* since 2015). He lives with his family in Zagreb.

Index